IT in Schools

A Handbook for Senior Managers

Edited by
Jim Donnelly

A QUESTIONS IT BOOK

ISBN 1 898149 35 6

First published in 1995 by
The Questions Publishing Company Ltd
27 Frederick Street
Hockley
Birmingham B1 3HH

Publication design
Andrew Moss Graphic Design

Printed by
BPC Wheatons Ltd, Exeter

The publishers would like to thank the National Council for Educational Technology for their contribution to this book. NCET publications mentioned in the text can be obtained from: NCET, Milburn Hill Road, Science Park, Coventry, CV4 7JJ.

Jim Donnelly *is the Head of Litherland High School, Sefton, Merseyside. He was a member of the School Curriculum and Assessment Authority (SCAA) Advisory Group on the revision of the National Curriculum. He is author of numerous books and articles on school management, including the management of information technology.*

Contents

IT in Schools

THE QUESTIONS

Introduction

We have all already witnessed some of the significant social and economic consequences of Information Technology (IT) and its impact on education. It is only possible to guess at a future when the whole process of schooling will be transformed, particularly as technologies which shift the focus and choice of the curriculum to the learner are further developed. At the same time we have a revised National Curriculum to implement!

It is very important to consider the future but managers need help now to make sense of IT and to deal with the realities of life in schools (shortage of technology and an even greater shortage of trained staff to use it). The purpose of this book is to raise the issues school managers are facing now and to provide practical guidance on how to deal with them.

The three main areas of concern are all addressed: the development of IT 'literacy', the power of IT to help deliver the National Curriculum and the use of IT in managing schools.

Part II provides examples of IT in use in some areas of the curriculum.

The power to transform the future for the next generation is - as always - in our hands. The responsibility is great, but so are the rewards.

Jim Donnelly
Litherland High School
May 1995

CHAPTER ONE

The Role of the Head Teacher and Senior Management Team

Jim Donnelly

The National Council for Educational Technology (NCET) is in a unique position to comment on the use of Information Technology (IT) in schools. Drawing on extensive research they conclude:

"The attitude of the head teacher is the most important factor in influencing attitudes towards computers and information technology in the school. Only if this attitude is positive will it be reflected in a positive attitude in the other teachers and pupils" *(IT works,* NCET, 1994, p.26*)*

They go on to point out that a "neutral or detached attitude towards computers is equivalent to a negative attitude". They emphasise that head teachers "can only give a positive lead in the use of IT in the curriculum and in the management of the school if they have an understanding of the value and use of IT".

The purpose of this book is to provide a senior school manager's guide to IT, with examples of what is being done in schools in this country. We start by looking at the key issues facing the head teacher and senior management team (SMT) in ensuring that their students gain the maximum learning benefits from the tools which are now available in the new information technology age.

The head teacher's support
There are five clear ways in which the support of the head teacher can be made visible.

1. The head teacher is seen to use IT in running the school and therefore acts as a role model. This can be made visible by the use of a laptop computer and/or a desk computer in the head's office, perhaps for word processing memos or for keeping spreadsheets of the school's day-to-day budget. This indicates to the rest of the staff that IT can be a tool for everyday work.

2. IT is given high status in the school by either the head or a (respected) member of the SMT taking an active and positive role in highlighting its importance. The IT co-ordinator needs to have easy access to this person and be seen to have this access. In some schools the IT co-ordinator is a member of the SMT at least for part of the time, but this of course will depend on the particular school's way of working.

3. There is a substantial budget available for the development of learning strategies using IT. This is possibly the most important way of making support clear. This budget should be 'ring-fenced' and subject to separate 'bid' procedures. Individual subject heads and teachers need to see that there will be a clear advantage to them in bidding for some of these resources, which means of course that once the resources have been allocated, they need to be backed up by the availability of training in their use.

It is also important that subject heads are asked to indicate what they are doing at present and how the additional resources will enhance learning in their subjects. In a primary school the money is likely to be allocated in a different way, but the principle of ring-fencing some for IT purposes is still important. The IT co-ordinator must be seen to have a strong influence in how resources are allocated.

4. INSET funds are allocated to provide IT training for staff.

5. IT is supported through the timetable. This can be done in a variety of ways, for example by requiring all departments to highlight their use of IT in their schemes of work and by providing teaching and/or technician time for which IT departments and teachers can bid.

The primary school

These points are at least as important for the head in a primary school. If s/he is not seen to provide a clear lead it is even more unlikely that the potential benefits of IT in enhancing children's learning will happen. Although the management structure is likely to be different, the key points are of crucial importance:

- using IT
- allocating financial and INSET resources to it

• enabling the IT co-ordinator to support other teachers

• asking how teachers are using IT.

The IT leader

There is a role for what is termed here the IT leader. This person may be the head or a member of the SMT; s/he may in some cases also be the IT co-ordinator. However the reason for specifically highlighting this role is that is important that the key strategic elements contained within it are addressed. It must therefore be clear who is to be responsible for the following:

Policy formulation

Someone has to take responsibility for ensuring that an IT policy for the school is developed. (The content of this policy is addressed on the next page)

Policy implementation

It is no good having a policy if it is only to be a notional kind of 'wish list'. It is important that someone keeps an eye on its implementation and at least makes regular attempts to evaluate its effectiveness.

Staff leadership

Someone needs to be responsible for leading staff (including subject departments in secondary schools) in the formulation of their own IT strategies.

Overall management of resources

There needs to be coherence in how IT is developed within the school, which includes the need to ensure that human and material resources are deployed to their best effect.

Key issues for senior managers

There are ten key issues which all senior managers in school must address. It is worth reiterating the point that the head teacher must be seen to be fully aware of - and supportive of - the way the school deals with the issues. The key issues are:

1. Formulation of a school IT policy
2. Purchasing IT equipment
3. Curriculum delivery and assessment
4. Management Information Systems
5. Co-ordinator - role and status

6. Technician support
7. Access for students and staff
8. Training in use of IT - INSET and other strategies
9. Security of data
10. Involvement of Governors and parents.

Issues 2, 3, 4, 5 and 9 are the subject of more detailed treatment later in the book. The other ones are dealt with now.

School IT policy

It is important that there is an agreed and understood policy on where IT fits within the school. Most schools find it useful to put this into writing but, as with all policies, what happens in practice is more important than whether it is written or not. With a clear policy it is easier for everyone to know where s/he fits into the development of IT and what will be possible over time. The following key elements need to be addressed in formulating such a policy.

Aims of IT, including the role of each department

These aims should relate to the primary purpose of the school, which is pupil learning. This will also include the use of management information systems and other facilities within the school office, even if it is only to say that they will be treated separately from the curricular uses of IT.

Present curricular provision

Include details of the part to be played by each subject teacher (or class teacher in the case of the primary school). A mapping exercise can be very informative and can serve to balance facts with hopes! The question of assessment of pupils' IT knowledge and skills needs to be addressed here.

Present resource provision

Include rooms, hardware, software, staff expertise and pupil resources. It is important that all provision is seen as belonging to the school and not to individual subject departments or class teachers. However, some 'ownership' of resources can increase their effective use - and certainly can stop them from falling into disrepair - so this needs to be interpreted with common sense.

Specific objectives

Include timescales for their achievement. Initially it may be difficult to set measurable objectives but over time the school does need to be more deliberate in planning. No set of written objectives should of course prevent something being done which becomes possible during the course of a year.

Resources

What will be made available during the timescales set for objectives? The more substantial the resources, the more potential there is for IT to develop within the school. However, it should always be borne in mind that the provision of resources does not necessarily of itself guarantee their effective use.

The role of the co-ordinator

Include status and salary; this is a crucial statement of intent, not only to help the development of IT within the school but also to prevent the co-ordinator from becoming frustrated at having to constantly justify and explain his/her position.

Review and evaluation procedures

This refers to the review and evaluation of the policy itself. One needs to indicate who will be involved in the review - the head should consider very carefully what the effect will be if s/he is not involved personally - and how the revised policy will be disseminated to staff.

Technician support

It is probably fair to say that computers are more robust and reliable in their working than they used to be. However, there are times when they need attention and this is where an IT technician is likely to be worth having. Many secondary schools have appointed technicians as a result of TVEI funding; primary schools have not had this benefit but as they use more computers they find an increasing need for at least part-time technician support. In the past LEAs were able to provide some centralised support but this provision is disappearing around the country.

Some schools are turning to leasing arrangements to help deal with this problem; newer computers and decent after-sales service can do a lot to offset the difficulties caused by machines breaking down. There is no easy solution. As with most aspects of Local Management of Schools it is necessary to sit down and work out the costs of technician support objectively. If the equipment is seen as important to pupil learning then 'down-time' (i.e. the time lost when the equipment is not working) is a significant part of the equation.

Problems with software can be eased by ensuring the use of similar packages across the school. Staff and pupil expertise can often sort out a problem caused by someone pressing the wrong key and not being able to get back to where s/he was!

One significant reason for having at least some technician support is to ensure that the teacher co-ordinator does not spend an inordinate amount of time trouble-shooting.

Access for students and staff

It is becoming clear that a key issue for the information technology age is going to be that of access. There are some concerns that those who can afford the technology will increase their advantage both economically and socially over those who cannot. This is clearly an issue for governments, both at a national and international level.

At the school level the issue is similar: how can we ensure that all pupils have access to the tools of learning? There are many potential barriers to this. One is that some staff will more readily embrace the new technologies than others; the school must address this issue in its curriculum planning to ensure that this does not happen. Until the arrival of CD-ROM - now also being used in primary schools and often being linked with the library or resource centre - there was some evidence that girls were not using the new technology as much as boys: the issue of gender imbalance obviously needs to be addressed.

The provision of separate computer rooms needs to be considered carefully, both in primary and secondary schools. In some cases there is so little room that there is not much scope for doing this. Where it can be done one needs to be careful to draw a correct balance between providing for pupils to use IT as and when appropriate - which suggests the need for computers in every classroom - while at the same time recognising that some computer skills need to be taught in a room where there are at least ten computers available.

Access to computers outside lesson time is also a key issue. If pupils are to be allowed to use computers freely some kind of supervision is necessary. Obviously it is wasteful to have expensive machinery used only during lesson times but any supervision is likely to incur

15

costs of some kind.

Decisions must be made on how staff will have access to the computers during lesson times. Do they have to book the room? Can they borrow equipment (as with televisions and video-recorders)? Can pupils be sent to a computer area on their own during lessons?

The other side of staff access is to do with staff being able to familiarise themselves with both hardware and software. Many schools are now buying laptop computers which staff can borrow to take home.

It is interesting to note that the NCET reports that "giving teachers easy access to computers encourages and improves the use of IT in the curriculum" (*IT works*, p.25).

Staff training

There is little doubt that staff training in the use of IT - and in the awareness of its potential for enhancing pupil learning - is crucial. All staff need training but their training needs are likely to be as individual as any class of children. Therefore, as far as possible, strategies need to be developed which will provide individual training. Fortunately computers themselves can to some extent help individualise this instruction. For example, most good word processing packages have a help facility which not only provides help with problems but also provides lessons on how to use the program.

Who is going to provide additional training? Will it be the co-ordinator (which will have timetabling implications in both primary and secondary schools) or will it be an outside body? Some LEAs can still provide training but this is by no means universal, nor is it guaranteed to last indefinitely. The school also has to decide how the training will be funded. If the training is going to benefit the pupils then there is an argument for the school funding it in total. Self-help should not be overlooked: one teacher (or member of a subject department) may be willing to share his/her expertise with colleagues.

Will the training be provided during school time and will cover be provided? Some can be done at lunchtimes and/or after school but who will provide it and who will stay for it? It is worth considering whether an overnight session for several staff at a hotel would not be cheaper (when the allowance for cover not needed is taken into account), less disruptive to pupils, more civilised and more conducive to real learning than sending a teacher off on a training course during a normal school day.

Again, it is important to look at the total costs of sending teachers on courses (including staff cover, travel and accommodation costs, not to mention that elusive thing known as quality of learning when the class has its own teacher) and compare it with the cost of providing laptops for staff to use as and when is convenient. This is where Local Management of Schools can be turned to advantage by a clear-sighted management team and governing body.

The final issue here is what the school does about the member of staff who needs training (if the children are to get their entitlement) but indicates no desire to take it. At some point the issue must be resolved.

Involvement of Governors and parents

It is important that the Governors of the school are aware of the changes in learning styles which result from the easy availability of IT. Their support will be needed if the right resources are to be allocated. They may also be able to help in other ways, bringing expertise (or even resources) to add to that of the school.

Parents, too, need to be kept up-to-date with what the school is doing. Parents' evenings provide a great opportunity to show some of the equipment which their children are using. They need to see how learning can be enhanced by using IT.

It might be well to end this first section in the same vein as it began, with another quote from the NCET publication, *IT works:*

"It needs the positive but democratic lead of the head teacher to ensure that IT is integrated into the schemes of work and programmes of study of the school."

This is what the Americans would call "an awesome responsibility"!

CHAPTER TWO

How Schools can Manage IT in the Curriculum

Jim Donnelly

The Dearing Review of the National Curriculum has clearly separated the delivery and assessment of Information Technology from that of Technology. The opportunity has also been taken to produce proposals which take account of some of the difficulties which schools had experienced with the original requirements. In this section we will look in brief at what IT now means in curricular terms; we will then deal with the practicalities of this for senior managers in schools who have to organise the timetabling of IT delivery and the intricacies of assessment.

Programmes of study

The IT programmes of study have been organised to pick out the main elements of IT capability and to develop them throughout the years of compulsory schooling. For each Key Stage there is a summary of purpose or focus.

Essential points for the senior manager

The detail of the IT programme of study is for the IT co-ordinator - however s/he is designated - to plan but there are a few essential points which senior managers need to understand.

1. Progression

The new proposals are designed to lead to pupils becoming autonomous learners by the end of Key Stage 3. Ideally this should be the culmination of nine years of use of IT and of pupils' development of IT capability. Each Key Stage has two main aspects which must be taught to pupils:

- communicating and handling information, and
- controlling and modelling (with the addition of monitoring at Key Stage 2 and measuring at Key Stages 3 and 4).

They are set out in this way so that a logical progression is clear. It is useful to remember that progression in terms of teaching is different to progression in terms of learning: IT as a subject of study lends itself particularly to an emphasis on the individual learner.

2. Entitlement

The IT entitlement as set out in the National Curriculum indicates a minimum entitlement for all pupils. It does not by any stretch of the imagination suggest that pupils are only capable of achieving this minimum but it does recognise that provision across the country is variable, due to differences in staff expertise, hardware and software availability and school commitment to IT. In an ideal world all pupils and staff would use IT across the curriculum, using its unique capacity to assist learning. The tools of IT would be as natural a part of every classroom as blackboards.

3. Expectations

The ever-changing nature of IT equipment leads to another point which is that today's expectations will need to be raised in the future. It is only a short while since a word processor was little more than an advanced form of typewriter. Nowadays it is possible to get simple packages which can be used by primary-age children to do their own newspapers or presentations.

Managing IT at Key Stages 1 and 2

Primary schools have an advantage when it comes to managing both the delivery and assessment of IT in the curriculum. Their normal way of working is to integrate several curricular demands into one piece of work. In simple terms this can be done with IT as easily as with, say, English or History. However, practical problems exist which make this more difficult than one would hope. First of all, very few teachers have been given up-to-date training in the use of IT, whether in initial teacher training or by the provision of suitable INSET. This is not to deny that much very valuable work has been done up and down the country: it is to say that in most schools teachers are not as familiar and comfortable with using IT as they need to be.

Summary of Purpose for each Key Stage

Key Stage 1

"Pupils should be taught to use IT equipment and software confidently and purposefully to communicate and handle information, and to support their problem solving, recording and expressive work."

Key Stage 2

"Pupils should be taught to extend the range of IT tools that they use for communication, investigation and control; become discerning in their use of IT; select information, sources and media for their suitability for purpose; and assess the value of IT in their working practices."

Key Stage 3

"Pupils should be taught to become critical and largely autonomous users of IT, aware of the ways in which IT tools and information sources can help them in their work; understand the limitations of such tools and of the results they produce; and use the concepts associated with IT systems and software and the associated technical terms."

Key Stage 4

"Pupils should be taught to develop greater responsibility for their use of IT; work competently and effectively with a range of IT tools and materials, acquiring an understanding of their more advanced features; and reflect critically on their own and others' use of IT."

By the end of Key Stage 3 it is hoped that pupils will have developed IT capability to the extent that they will be able to use it to enhance learning across the curriculum which they study at Key Stage 4.

Even if the staff are willing and have some degree of expertise the provision of suitable hardware and software is patchy. It will be some time before the situation approaches the ideal and in the meantime each school has to do the best it can to provide all children with the best IT entitlement it can.

Most primary schools have appointed an IT co-ordinator (more will be said about co-ordinators in Chapter 5) and in this way they are gradually developing expertise. It is worth emphasising that IT will not achieve its full potential until every teacher and every pupil sees it as just another tool for learning, albeit an extremely powerful one.

The Dearing Review gave a notional time for each subject, which at Key Stage 1 was 27 hours (per child per year) and at Key Stage 2 was 36 hours. This figure was for the guidance of the Advisory Group and in most primary schools the delivery of IT may not be something which it will be useful to time.

Assessment will be the key to checking whether IT capability has been achieved and teachers will need clear and detailed support in being able to check if their children are performing as well as comparable children elsewhere. Non-statutory guidance will be important for schools, particularly with examples of what children at different ages should be able to do.

Managing IT at Key Stage 3

While at Key Stages 1 and 2 the notional hours allocated to IT will not necessarily lead to problems, the matter is not as simple at Key Stage 3. Once the Dearing Review set out the notional Key Stage timings for Advisory Groups, an expectation was created that subjects would need that amount of time for delivery. Thus an allocation of 45 hours for IT was seen to represent a need for a 'double' lesson (in a 40-period week) for the subject on the timetable. The subsequent guidance is that half of this time will be needed to teach IT skills and half of it will be used for the application of these skills across the curriculum.

However Dearing has made clear that it is up to schools to decide how the curriculum (in all subjects) is to be delivered. In practical terms, this gives schools three choices for IT: first, they can allocate a 'double' lesson for delivery and assessment; secondly, they can allocate a 'single' lesson (or its equivalent during the Key Stage); thirdly, they can try to deliver and assess IT totally across the curriculum. There are examples of each of these strategies being adopted by schools which have satisfied OFSTED inspectors.

Assessment issues

It can be useful to start Key Stage 3 planning by looking at the need for assessment. The school's management team needs to consider how IT will be assessed at the end of the Key Stage and how the school can ensure that the pupils have reached the required level of capability. The school which allocates the equivalent of a 'double' period per week will find this easier to do. If the teaching is clear and other subject areas are developing their use of IT then examples of pupils' work will be readily available for inclusion in a 'portfolio'. It is good practice to involve the pupils as far as possible in gathering this portfolio evidence so that, for example, if they are doing a particular piece of work in English which requires them to do some desktop publishing they would then bring this work - or an extra copy of it - to the IT teacher for inclusion in their portfolio.

If the school decides on the equivalent of one period per week for teaching then there are various ways of doing this. One solution is to have a double lesson in one or two of Years 7, 8 and 9 with no timetabled time for the other year(s) of the Key Stage; another one is to operate a modular programme, combining IT with some elements of Technology or PSE to allow for one-hour inputs on a 'circus' basis. There is no doubt that schools can deliver IT in this way but it does put extra strains on the person(s) responsible for assessing IT at the end of the Key Stage. It is also the case that the best time to allocate the double (because of assessment) would be in Year 9, which is precisely when the need for time for other subject areas (e.g. a second modern foreign language) is at its most pressing.

Some schools actually deliver and assess IT without any separate input. In some ways this would be the ideal solution, but so also would be the delivery of, say, English in this way: the fact that this does not generally happen is an indication of the difficulties inherent in this approach. However if schools can manage it this way - and allocate the personnel and equipment resources to ensure OFSTED are satisfied - then they are at liberty to do so.

It is important that senior managers realise that children reaching

Key Stage 3 in the immediate future are unlikely to have had the opportunities for using IT in the primary school (for reasons already suggested) to the extent which is desirable, and allowance may need to be made for this.

Managing Key Stage 4

There is an assumption at Key Stage 4 that pupils will develop their IT capability across the curriculum. This does presuppose that pupils will have become autonomous learners by the end of Key Stage 3 - which may not be achievable in the near future.

Individual schools are at liberty, of course, to timetable IT for all pupils at Key Stage 4 - either regularly or as part of a 'circus' with other subjects - but the National Curriculum does not require this to happen.

Implications

Several key issues in the delivery of IT in the curriculum have been alluded to already. Senior managers in both primary and secondary schools will in particular need to think about their response to the following questions:

- How will IT be delivered in our school?
- How will it be assessed? (It is not enough to ensure that every pupil spends a certain amount of time using a computer; s/he needs to know how to repeat the exercise!)
- How will the entitlement of every pupil be achieved? (In particular, how will girls be given equal access?)
- How will the need for IT training for all staff be achieved? How will staff become aware of the potential for IT for pupil learning?
- How will the hardware and software be made available? How will an increasing expectation by parents to see IT in use be met?

Finally - but most importantly - how will we prepare our pupils for a society in which IT is causing both a learning revolution and a far-reaching change in society, one which is comparable in many ways to that caused by the Industrial Revolution in the 18th century?

CHAPTER THREE

Creating Autonomous Learners

Francis Howlett

A ll teachers want their pupils to become autonomous learners. They love to impart knowledge to their charges, but they also want pupils to learn the study skills which are essential if they are to function as independent learners. IT can have an important role to play in this process.

A safe and non-threatening environment

We all learn from our mistakes, and yet the fear of being wrong hampers many learners from taking the first steps towards independent learning. Learners should feel safe in what they are doing, should be encouraged to experiment without fear of ridicule, and should receive immediate feedback in the form of praise, encouragement or gentle correction. The good teacher will always try to provide this kind of environment: IT can be used as an additional tool for meeting this aim.

Learners who have problems with writing and presentation can have their work improved by the computer. They can try out different ways of writing words and sentences without worrying about crossings out. They can discuss their work with the teacher or with their peers at the drafting stage. Mistakes in spelling and grammar can be easily corrected and the final results can look as good as anyone else's. Pupils who might otherwise be ashamed of their work can take a pride in presentation. Gaining self-esteem is often the first stage towards autonomous learning.

Learners with short memories or low attention spans find it hard to learn from corrected work unless there is virtually no delay between doing the work and seeing the corrections. Computer programs which provide instant positive feedback when the work is going well and assistance when problems are met can help pupils make significant progress.

Pupils do not need to expose their weaknesses to the whole class: mistakes can be made, and only the pupil and the computer need know. The computer does not become impatient, it does not deride or belittle, it can allow repeated attempts, it can give a second chance. Pupils who feel they need to repeat work can do so without holding back the rest of the class.

There are suggestions that some pupils can make faster progress with the computer because they no longer fear pressure from their classmates not to do well.

Richer source materials

There is no immediate prospect of IT replacing traditional sources of information such as dictionaries, encyclopaedias, art books - indeed, it will often be the role of IT sources to lead the pupil to such paper-based resources. IT, particularly in the form of CD-ROM and inter-active video, has made a wealth of material available, necessitating the acquisition of sophisticated information handling skills.

For instance, pupils will often need to look at newspaper articles for information to support a topic. Newspapers on CD-ROM allow a pupil to see how a topic has developed over a year, or to compare its treatment in several newspapers. Text can be easily incorporated in a report: the pupil spends more time on analysis, because time spent copying quotes has been reduced to a bare minimum.

Pupils consulting large databases such as encyclopaedias or news-papers soon learn that the skills of grouping, organising and classifying are vital. For instance, searching on the word 'Ireland' in a year's sup-ply of newspapers is not very satisfactory if the subject being studied is Ireland's role in the European Union, or the progress of Ireland's foot-ball team. Pupils soon learn that finding lots of information is unhelp-ful, and that narrower, more focused, searches are needed.

By comparing the treatment of a topic in different newspapers or encyclopaedias, pupils can be encouraged to distinguish between fact and opinion, to question the validity of what they are reading, and to make judgements about bias. It is only when they can question critically the information they are receiving that they can become fully autonomous learners.

Above all, these electronic sources give pupils access to information which would otherwise be difficult to find, and can present it in ways which are easy for the pupil to use. For instance, instead of being faced with page after page of similar-looking text or pictures, a good search strategy will take the student directly to the information required. Well-constructed CD-ROMs will give cross-references which the more adventurous can explore, each of these cross-references leading to further context-based experiences.

Most important of all, the pupils are in control, finding out what they want, not dealing with what has been provided in a textbook. The pupils are engaged in original research, with the very real possibility that they will find something that surprises not only themselves but their teacher. This can happen even with very young children, as in the case of the seven-year-olds who were searching an encyclopaedia to find all the instruments of the orchestra in the brass family, and surprised their teacher by discovering that the Chinese gong, while made of brass, is in the percussion family.

Presenting, analysing and interpreting data

There are many curricular activities such as surveys, experiments and investigations which involve the pupil in collecting and presenting data. All too often the production of the graph or chart has been the end point of the exercise, rather than the beginning. Of course pupils need to learn how to draw bar charts, pie charts and other kinds of graphs. But once these skills have been learned, interest should shift from the drawing of the graph to its interpretation. Pupils in a history lesson, for example, might enter details of gender and age at death from local parish records or from gravestones. This can lead to some very nice graph work which will satisfy many pupils, but the truly independent learner will investigate further, making hypotheses about life-expectancy in different times, and test these against the data.

Spreadsheets, databases and other graphing packages on a computer allow the pupil to enter the data and then present it in a variety of ways. The pupil can decide the most suitable way of showing results without the tedious need for drawing new graphs. Similarly, different sets of data can be combined or compared, so that one pupil's results can become part of a much wider picture, whether that of the pupil's own class or at a national or international level.

In scientific experiments the use of datalogging equipment can be particularly beneficial. Pupils can record data over very long periods (hours, days or longer) or over very short periods (several measurements in a second) which would be impossible by hand. Previously they have had to rely upon other people's data in such experiments. Moreover, dataloggers allow the data to be input directly into the graphing package, eliminating transcription errors and taking the pupil immediately to the interpretation of the data.

Experiments can be repeated if the data is unsatisfactory, whereas with manual methods the amount of time spent in collecting the data and producing graphs makes this impossible. Indeed experiments, such as those using motion sensors or heat sensors attached to a computer through a control box, can provide immediate graphs which will allow the pupils to see the effects of changes as they happen. This makes it easier for the pupils to understand the graph, and helps them make inferences about the experiment and the scientific concepts they are studying.

Analytical and divergent thinking

Above all, information technology can provide the pupil with a safe environment in which to try out different ideas. This might be quite simply trying out different endings or orders in a piece of creative writing, or it might involve making use of spreadsheets and simulations with their powerful facilities for asking questions such as 'What would happen if ...?' All pupils should have the chance to do some computer modelling, whether it involves using ready-made simulation programs or it is something that the pupils have developed themselves. Such opportunities will help the pupils to develop analytical methods and allow them to explore divergent ideas. The teacher cannot be sure where such investigations will take the pupil, but this is a risk which we must take if we are to trust our pupils as autonomous learners.

Francis Howlett is a Programme Manager at the National Council for Educational Technology

CHAPTER FOUR

Using IT for Assessment

Lesley Glover

D uring 1993/4, the National Council for Educational Technology conducted an IT and assessment project. The aims were to raise awareness of the potential of computer assisted assessment and to offer guidance to developers, administration planners and policymakers. The project included an exploration of the packages available, a survey of current uses of IT to support assessment and a conference to identify key issues and future developments.

Assessment issues

This project has identified issues that will help those either about to begin using computer assisted assessment (CAA) or updating what they already have. The information comes from those in primary and secondary education who have already travelled some distance along this path.

CAA includes all aspects of the use of computers for assessment, from recording results to computer delivered examinations. The table on the next page shows some areas where computers might be used in assessment.

Current use and developments

NCET surveyed schools known to be using CAA in some form, to find out what they thought about these systems.

Predominantly, the main use of CAA is for recording and reporting, with 35% of respondents using CAA data to identify changes in student performance. A wide range of different packages were used, many of which support specialist subject areas. These were mainly sci-

Where might computers find a place in assessment?		
Diagnostic Assessment	Supporting Self assessment	Screening/ identifying needs for remedial provision
Access to assessment for students with special needs	Providing immediate feedback to students and teachers	Supporting remote assessment
Tracking progress	Collating and recording results	Reporting to parents
Examining IT skills	Formative and summative tests	Computerised examinations

ence, closely followed by mathematics, geography and IT. When asked about the uses of IT across the institution, record keeping was the predominant reply (nearly 80%). Approximately two-thirds used IT for reports for parents and for supporting achievement records. The other main reported uses were:

• Monitoring changes in student performance
• Producing statistical returns (for LEA, DFE, etc.)
• Diagnosing student learning needs
• Assessing competence
• Testing
• Making decisions on future learning needs
• Action planning
• Identifying students at risk academically
• Assessing the interests and aptitudes of students
• Assessing prior learning

We also found some innovative uses of CAA. Some examples are given below of how some institutions in the survey are using IT for assessment.

A further education college has been using computers for their students to take examinations in the BTEC National Diploma in

Computing. It appears to have been a positive experience for the students, who reported that it had been "a more relaxing way of taking exams than the traditional way".

A project now underway in a group of schools is evaluating the benefits of a programme which provides training in phonic skills for children and adults who have difficulties in learning to read. The programme assesses and profiles individual strengths and weaknesses, provides immediate feedback to students and maintains detailed records of all work undertaken.

Computerised tests

Interest is growing in the potential of computerised adaptive tests. So far, wherever these systems have been demonstrated, educators have given them a warm welcome. In a series of seminars held last year, primary and secondary heads considered the potential of a US system. They said that a system tailored to the National Curriculum in England would be most welcome. In particular they suggested that a skills assessment programme that reflected an individual school's view on which skills should be assessed, and when, would be particularly helpful. They liked the idea that pupils could assess themselves at any particular time, in a way that did not disturb the rest of the class. The facility to assess at the beginning of the year, throughout the year, and at the end, was also desirable. Support was voiced for a common skills marking assessment particularly for use at the point of transfer between schools. This includes pupils arriving part-way through a year, as well as wholesale transfer from one phase to another, including entry to post-16 institutions.

Benefits

Survey respondents identified saving staff time, ease of analysis of results, the provision of a unified assessment framework and support for national assessment requirements as positive advantages. Also, computer assisted assessment was said to provide objective information on student performance. School staff comment on the high quality of output available and the value of this in reporting to outside agencies. One school reported that the "...package, has helped us to produce relevant standardised reports to parents in an attractive professional format". Another said that "use of a particular report writing package has saved a lot of time as staff complete OMR (optical mark reader) sheets rather than writing full reports. But these are only as good as the textfile that is used to generate them and much time and expertise is required to produce good quality personal textfiles".

Difficulties

The main difficulties in using computer assisted assessment were said to be lack of staff training and the time required to input data. Schools also reported problems with software, and a lack of computers for staff and students. Some schools have experienced difficulties with implementing systems to record and report on National Curriculum assessment when the requirements were regularly being changed.

Effects of computerised assessment

We asked our survey respondents what they felt the main effects of CAA to have been on teaching and learning. They replied that:

- assessment can be made available at the time and place of student need (47%)
- feedback from assessment can be used to improve teacher performance (41%)
- teaching becomes more targeted on assessment (42%).

Minorities report that computer assisted assessment supports better differentiated courses for students (12%) and 10% report direct curriculum change as a result of CAA. One school argued that "... it helps to clarify goals and also provides useful feedback on teaching materials". Another said: "we have noticed increased student motivation, and pupil IT skills have improved".

Cost effectiveness of CAA

The cost effectiveness of these systems is not easily quantifiable. For example, how is the quality of assessment information or student motivation measured? Most educational institutions from the survey would, however, say that CAA, as a device for record keeping, reporting and analysis is "cost effective" compared to paper-based systems. CAA offers a flexible device for providing feedback so that reporting systems can be tailored to meet the different needs of students, parents, education authorities and employers.

It also offers new opportunities for test delivery. Tests can be regularly updated to improve reliability without the risk of introducing bias into the selection of items to suit the testing mode. The assessment of students at the time of need, without the demand for special facilities, can free up teaching timetables whilst improving pupils' motivation and possibly performance. However, one school stated that, "staff do not like writing objective test questions and find it time consuming".

Choosing what to buy

We asked the survey respondents what advice they could give to prospective purchasers of CAA. One senior teacher advised on developing a whole school concept of what using IT for assessment and recording achievement would actually mean. He also said that given the opportunity to start again, "We would have spent more money on staff support". This school had actually split their resources in an 80:20 ratio, 80% on hardware and software and 20% on staff support. He felt this should have been on a 50:50 basis instead.

One head teacher advised that it is imperative to make sure that all systems in the school are compatible: "Record keeping should be compatible with the administration system and an integral part of individual teacher recording," he stressed.

Another head teacher warned that "the use of IT for assessment should be a slave not a master to the teacher".

When asked what information would have helped them, the majority of our survey respondents (over 40%) said they would have appreciated some case studies of good practice. Over 40% were interested in codes of practice. Information was also requested on the types of packages and systems available.

Thus, from our survey and interviews we have devised a decision-making checklist for prospective purchasers of CAA, which is included in our latest report, *Using IT for Assessment: going forward*, which is available free from NCET.

Where next?

From our research we know that there is a great deal of interest in the development of using computers for assessment and a strong need for

34

The school may well decide that the IT co-ordinator will carry all these responsibilities, in which case it is almost certain that s/he will be a member of the senior management team of the school. The job description of the IT co-ordinator needs to make clear whether s/he is to carry out some or all of these senior manager responsibilities. In addition, the following responsibilities need to be covered:

Leading the technology

With the ever-changing nature of IT the school needs to have someone who knows what is available and to whom staff can turn for ideas for the future.

Mapping the technology

This links in with the senior manager's responsibility for the overall management of resources. The investment in IT equipment is high in both small and large schools and someone needs to be able to monitor how effectively it is used.

Purchase of equipment

When one is spending a large amount of money on equipment and on-site licences, worthwhile savings can be made by having a person who is knowledgeable about the market. Being able to spend money wisely means that total costs, including likely running costs (maintenance, toner, paper, etc.), need to be carefully identified and monitored.

Technical support

This will vary from the ability to put right a piece of hardware to showing staff how to get themselves out of difficulties with the software. If this is to be done by a teacher then it is important that the limits of the facility are made clear to all staff. It is not really acceptable for teachers to regularly leave their own classes on a 'fire fighting' operation in some other classroom. (See also Chapter 1)

Staff training and general in-house support

There is not much point in having powerful equipment if staff are not able to use it. It may be worth noting that all training does not need to be provided by one person. Schools may be able to call on outside expertise, some of which may be free (for example from an LEA support team or from a supplier). The knowledge available among the school's own staff should not be underestimated; for example, some of the administration staff may be able to train teaching staff in the use of software packages.

Collecting pupils' work and ensuring that it is assessed

This is particularly important at the end of key stages where schools will be expected to produce evidence of pupil progress for OFSTED.

Network manager

Most secondary schools have at least one computer network - even if only for the administration of the school - and many primary schools also have similar set-ups. It is necessary to have a clear idea of how networks will be managed. They are potentially very powerful but experience suggests that the more powerful the system the more things can go wrong - and the worse the problems when they do!

System design and maintenance

Once the school has several computers it is worth thinking of them as a system. The decisions about how these are to be maintained need to be constantly evaluated and updated. A system manager will mean different things to different people: for example, in some schools it will refer to the person who manages the administration network, who may or may not be a member of the teaching staff.

Present practice

The practice in schools varies considerably. In one school the IT co-ordinator simply collects and co-ordinates the work of the pupils. In another the co-ordinator undertakes mainly a training and support role. In yet another it is the technical side of IT which is the focus of the job. Whatever the emphasis of the role, it needs to be clearly inter-twined with the overall development and focus of the school. The IT co-ordinator in the future will increasingly be a key figure as teaching and learning styles change. A 'techie', selected purely on the basis of technical know-how, will not necessarily be able to give the lead which this changing situation will require.

In moving to a new definition of the role of the IT co-ordinator it may be useful to identify three key areas of development:

- IT as an administration tool, helping to make the school more effective at delivering education.
- IT as a tool for learning, helping pupils to learn faster and more effectively.
- IT as a subject in its own right, with its own intrinsic value and

examination success.

The positions of the IT leader, the IT co-ordinator and the other members of the IT team (teaching staff, technicians, administration staff) need to be set within this context. Once that is done the positions of all other staff then need to be determined!

The IT co-ordinator's skills

Given the nature of the job it is unlikely that the IT co-ordinator will be able to function in the future without the following:

- Skills in using a computer, preferably including detailed knowledge of operating systems.
- Organisational skills, both to map the curriculum and to fulfil the demands of the National Curriculum.
- Managerial skills, working with the IT leader (if this is a separate person) to ensure that the best use is made of IT resources.
- Interpersonal skills, to ensure that staff feel confident in approaching the co-ordinator for advice.

Without these skills the school will find that other staff are reluctant to become involved in the development of IT. Although some co-ordinators will possess these skills in varying balances, in the best schools s/he will have all of them.

The following questions may help to focus the school's response to the task of clarifying the IT co-ordinator's role:

- What exactly is the nature of his/her job?
- What knowledge does s/he have of both hardware and software?
- Who will perform the technician and/or troubleshooting role?
- What is the co-ordinator's status, measured in terms of salary and access to the key decision-making structures in the school?
- How much time is needed for the task?
- What is his/her staff training role?

The IT co-ordinator is a key figure in ensuring that IT is developed fully in a school. It is important that senior management recognises this.

John Bradshaw is Head of Information Technology at Litherland High School, Sefton, Merseyside.

CHAPTER SIX

Management Information Systems

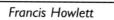

Francis Howlett

S chools are bombarded with manufacturers' fliers claiming that their management information system is the best. How are schools to decide? Before making any changes, the school management team should stop and ask some serious questions. These questions will fall into three basic categories:

What are our present information outputs?

For example, do we have financial reports, class lists, school reports, records of achievement, room and staff allocation, timetable, attendance, exam entries, DFE statistics, library usage?

What are our present information inputs?

For example, do we have LEA information, feeder school information, staff hand-written lists, registers, OMR (optical mark reader) forms, back-of-envelope calculations, library cards?

What are our present and future needs?

For example, do we want to use staff and accommodation more cost-effectively, free administrative staff to allow them to help teaching staff, improve appearance of reports, improve pupil tracking, cut down absenteeism?

Before changing existing practices, schools should conduct a 'needs analysis'. This might involve calling in a firm of consultants or asking every member of staff questions like those outlined above. Whatever method is chosen, the impetus must come from the head teacher and the senior management team. The whole staff must be involved at every stage, both before the needs analysis is carried out, during the analysis and afterwards, when changes are considered.

The analysis might indicate that only a few simple changes need to be made to existing procedures; very small schools might not need a computerised MIS at all. Or it might be that the school has very little idea of how its information flows. Computerising an already chaotic or unclear system can only make things worse. Most schools are somewhere between these two extremes, and will find that many existing procedures can be improved with little cost.

Software

What do the different systems have to offer? The two key elements are finance and pupil records.

A good finance package can help with current expenditure and forward planning. Tailor-made reports can be produced for purposes such as departmental accounts, planning meetings, governors, auditors. Many heads will want to use the system to try out different budgetary solutions such as exploring the effects of making different savings or commitments. IT makes easy the 'What if ...?' approach to financial planning. However, some schools have found the financial modules supplied with their system far too restrictive, and many smaller schools will find a simple spreadsheet adequate. for their needs.

The extent to which a school is tied into the LEA's accounting methods must also be considered. Does the school have to follow set procedures which have been built into the module supplied by the LEA? Are financial details sent to and from the LEA via an e-mail link? This will limit the school's scope for experimentation. Although few schools are responsible for the staff payroll, having the information about staff cost is vital for financial planning.

With regard to the other main use of MIS, pupil records, the bottom line is that any system used must be accurate and able to record and reflect properly each child's attainment and progress.

Quality of information

The quality of the information held on the central records determines the usefulness of the system. It must be accurate, up-to-date and transferable. Some systems are very inflexible, with tedious procedures for entering data. Others are a delight to use. Often this will be a matter of personal preference, so consultation is vital. How easy is it for different members of staff to add data? Can the system cope with pupils who are not in traditional two-parent families? How easily does it cope with exceptions? Are staff so familiar with the idiosyncrasies of the existing software that they no longer present a problem? (If the school has invested a considerable amount of time training staff it may be that the present system is actually more effective than a new system which will require new training.)

A good system will be flexible enough to allow any combinations of pupil details to be printed out according to need. Poor software will restrict the school to what the system thinks is needed. Different people (pastoral or subject heads, form teachers, deputies) will want to use the information for different purposes. Can subsets of data be taken off the system for detailed work? Are there safeguards against having different versions of the data simultaneously?

Special Educational Needs

Keeping track of pupils with special needs provides yet another opportunity for using the system to predict future curriculum and staffing or resources needs. The availability of good quality information is often a necessary precondition for future action.

Statistical returns

The ability of a system to perform, as if by magic, the irksome chore of producing statistical returns, such as Form 7, make this a very welcome feature. Make sure your system will do exactly what is required by your government department.

Timetabling

Some timetabling modules can build a timetable, some are only capable of checking and displaying. If a school is already happy with its timetabling package, it is important to check that the details can be fed from the stand-alone package into the main system.

A good timetabling package can be an enormous time-saver, allowing several versions to be generated at the planning stage. A completely new timetable can be generated during the school year if needed, something which was unimaginable in larger schools before the advent of IT solutions. The better packages will allow individual timetables to be printed for staff, rooms, pupils, subjects and faculties.

Staff cover

For some reason, teachers are often more willing to accept computer-allocated substitutions because they feel that in the long run the computer will be fairer (or less biased) than the deputy in charge of cover.

Financial and curriculum planning

This is an area where IT can allow schools to try out a whole variety of different plans before committing themselves.

Attendance

There are several ways of using IT to keep track of pupil attendance, and the school need not be tied to the module supplied with the MIS. Can the attendance package link into the MIS? Does it take data off the pupil records? Can it be used to update pupil records? Can data be input electronically, say through bar code readers, swipe cards or optical mark readers?

Personnel records

This module holds the records of all staff. This should link in to the finance module if the school is responsible for pay.

Examinations and assessment

Many schools will need a module which can take pupil and subject data off the main system and turn it into the format required by the examination board. Some of these modules perform statistical analysis on the results and can also provide statistics on pupil destinations. Transfer of exam data entries to the exam boards is via floppy disc or e-mail.

National Curriculum assessment

This module offers enormous scope for cutting down administrative chores if it can take pupil data off the main system and feed results back to pupil records, as well as providing the statistics required for parents, the DFE and the LEA.

NCET's booklet on assessment, *Using IT for Assessment (February 1994)*, lists all 31 currently known assessment software packages, their basic facilities, suppliers and price structures. It is available for £3.50 from the Information Officer at NCET.

Profiling, Records of Achievement and report writers

These may be part of the main system or purchased separately. Will this require all the pupil data to be keyed in again? Will it take names and details from the system and allow the finished reports to be fed back into pupil records? Will the report writer allow rapid entry of details using OMR? Does it have a spell checker?

Comment banks can lead to the production of very similar and stylised reports. Many schools find they need to rewrite the comment banks supplied with their system. This can entail an enormous amount of work, but if it is undertaken in a co-operative manner it can lead to an increased sense of ownership and pride.

Library housekeeping systems

Very few schools have a library system that is linked to the MIS. Will it be necessary to key in all the pupil data again? There is an enormous amount of work in keying in the data on thousands of books, yet most bibliographic data is already available in electronic format, for instance on CD-ROM: can the system take in such data?

A good library system can give information on patterns of use, and assist in resource management. An electronic catalogue can offer far greater flexibility for searching than going through cards. Pupils and teachers will need to be trained in how to use such a resource. It is not absolutely essential to use the Library module provided with the school MIS system, provided that all the necessary data (particularly names of students and staff) can be 'downloaded' and put into the new software package.

Implications of MIS for the school

Having an MIS and using it to best effect means ensuring security for the data, easy access for teachers and training.

Security

Make sure you ask the following questions:

- How would you cope with a partial or complete loss of data?
- How long can you manage without access to your system?
- What would happen if there was a major fire, a malicious attack on the main computer or an attack on the data held in it?
- Is your system secure against unauthorised access?

Passwords should be changed frequently; machines and equipment which hold sensitive data should be secure against theft and unauthorised entry. Copies of all data should be made at frequent intervals and stored off-site. Contingency arrangements, perhaps with a neighbouring school, should be made in case of breakdown.

Access and accommodation

Where is the best place to site the MIS computers? If you want the staff to use the system it must be easy for them to access it. If you only have one MIS computer, how can the head work on curriculum planning while the secretary is updating pupil records or the bursar is doing the accounts? If you are going to have an MIS network, which areas of the school should be networked?

It is possible to have a very flexible system which is not networked if data is transferred to different machines on floppy discs, but this carries the danger of ending up with different versions of the data. Some heads and deputies swear by their laptop computer, using it to do administrative work wherever and whenever they want.

Hardware

The choice of hardware should be considered after the decisions have been taken on software. Most schools find that they soon need more machines, more storage space on the server, more printers or a larger network. There should be early planning for expansion and upgrading, with an in-built review procedure.

Staffing

Introducing an MIS will bring about changes in the structure of the school. A secretary who previously typed letters and looked after the dinner money might now find herself in charge of the administrative infrastructure of the school. A deputy who used to spend half a year building the timetable and allocating staff for cover now finds the machine will help do this quickly and efficiently. The power centre of the school will shift, and schools must be ready for these changes.

Staff development and support

There is never enough time for training, but without it the system will not be used efficiently. Training must be built into the school's development plan. What will happen when staff who run the system leave?

The role of the head teacher

Where MIS is being used effectively, head teachers are directly involved in leading developments and ensuring quality use of the system. They are using the system themselves and encouraging staff through consultation, training and providing easy access. The commitment of the head is vital to success.

Francis Howlett is a Programme Manager at the National Council for Educational Technology.

CHAPTER SEVEN

Computers and the Law

Siobhan Wharton

The falling prices of personal computers and improving ease of use have resulted in significant growth in the use of electronic information to assist us in all aspects of our life; the education environment is no exception - in fact, it is more demanding than the commercial environment due to curriculum and budget pressures requiring excellent value for money and exceptional flexibility.

We have evolved from a mainframe computer environment into the personal computer age; intelligent workstations can give us direct personal interaction with distributed information sources; large amounts of information can be stored and manipulated quickly and easily.

This degree of flexibility and accessibility brings new responsibilities to those who handle personal information. The modern digital computer is also capable of making limitless copies of information without generation losses. Furthermore, this information is compact, and can be moved around very easily and quickly - data held on a floppy disk can be copied very easily and successive copies are flawless duplicates of the original. Compare this with current audio, video and paper media, where successive copies are devalued by reductions in quality.

As a result of all these changes, more individuals are finding themselves affected by new working practices and legislation.

The principles of copyright

The fundamental principle of copyright is very simple: an individual or body who creates or produces an original intellectual work should have the sole right to determine how it is used within society and they may demand payment in return for permission to use their work. In being able to benefit financially, the creator is encouraged to produce material for the benefit of others and the whole of society benefits as a result.

A copyright offence is committed when anyone copies a work without the creator's agreement with the intention of depriving them of the right to benefit from their work. UK copyright laws are among the most strict in the world, and significantly favour the copyright holder. Copyright is also covered by international treaties that ensure copyright works are effectively protected worldwide.

The penalties for infringement of copyright are potentially very serious. Liabilities can amount to unlimited fines, or imprisonment. This applies not only to the individual who commits the offence, but also to responsible individuals such as company directors, trustees, and possibly governors and head teachers if it is deemed that they may have given consent for copyright infringement. The best means of ensuring this cannot happen is for responsible bodies to set out a policy, or code of conduct relating to copyright and to ensure that accurate records of licences are kept.

The scope of the Copyright Act

The Copyright Act recognises many categories of work. Indeed, what is apparently a single entity may consist of many individual copyrights. For example, a music CD will include a large number of copyrights relating to the:

- individual musical works
- individual literary works (in the form of lyrics)
- sound recording of the music and lyrics
- published edition comprising the arrangement of tracks on the CD, lyrics and illustrations

So, even a simple CD may contain many copyrights. Each of these copyrights may be owned by different people or bodies. Unlike patents, there is no copyright register; finding out who owns a particular copyright can be very difficult!

Different classes of work have different protections under the Act. The period of protection for the majority of works will be at least 50 years. Once a copyright has expired, the work becomes public domain (but published editions of the work will carry a new copyright). It may appear that anything and everything is protected, even an idle doodle on a piece of paper. However, cases bought over such trivial works have been refused protection. A work must have required some expenditure of time, effort, talent or money to create something worth protecting.

It is important to recognise that the copyright and the physical item are distinct. If you buy a painting, you do not automatically buy the right to copy it. If you wished to do so, you would need to negotiate a separate agreement with the copyright owner; this may not even be the painter, if the copyright has previously been sold to someone else. The Copyright Act recognises certain concessions that do allow you to copy without infringing. There are both general concessions and special educational concessions. These provisions allow limited copies of materials to be made for private study or examination purposes. (Note that the provisions are the subject of recent change and schools need to read the details of the new concessions carefully.)

These concessions cannot be cited in cases where the rights of use have been explicitly restricted by a licence, for example a software licence.

Single user licences

Computer programs are treated as literary works under the Copyright Act. In the vast majority of cases, the right to use a copy of a computer program is granted via a licence. The software licence grants limited rights to use a program and its documentation. It is important to recognise that when you buy a software package, you are buying the:

- licence to use a copy of the program and documentation
- media on which the program and documentation are distributed.

Most software standalone licences grant you the right to install a copy of the software on a hard disk and to make one backup copy for safe keeping.

You need to have a licence for each copy of a software program. If you buy a single user licence and install copies on more than one hard disk, you are infringing the licence agreement. (Note however, that some licences grant you the right to make a copy for use on one machine at home as well as at work).

A licence is normally required for each version of a program. It is important to keep any licence agreements safe for two reasons, firstly, it may be required to prove you are legally licensed and, secondly, upgrade licences are often significantly lower in cost than new licences (but require some proof of the original purchase).

Although the information presented here has referred to programs, it applies equally to data, such as in a CD-ROM encyclopaedia, although in some of these cases, limited rights may be granted to take copies of small amounts of the data for study òr personal use.

Network/site licences.

Most standard off-the-shelf software packages are licensed for a single user and do not allow sharing or networking use. Specific licences are required to network software. You must have a valid licence for every copy of a program being used on a network, even if the program is not being stored on a disk at the station. This is especially important with the emergence of informal peer-to-peer networks; it is illegal to share a single-user licensed product across a number of systems!

Licences that allow multiple copies of a program to be used are becoming more common. It is no longer unusual to buy a 10-user version of a program that consists of a 10-user licence agreement only (without any distribution media). This licence would allow you to copy legally or share an existing program between ten 10 PCs.

Summary

- The Copyright Act exists to protect the interest of creators of works.
- Copyright applies to all of the software being used today; rights to use software are granted by the purchase of a software licence.
- There are important distinctions between single user and network licensed products that must be considered when connecting PCs together.
- Educational concessions in the Copyright Act do not generally apply to software.
- Copies of software licence agreement and any upgrades must be kept safely and correct legal use of software monitored and controlled.

Some software vendors are becoming more aggressive in defence of their copyrights; this has been demonstrated by a number of FAST actions recently.

The use of multimedia brings many new copyright issues into school, including questions of how and when to seek permission for materials extracted from a wide variety of sources. Unfortunately, there is insufficient space to spend on complex issues here. The National Council for Educational Technology has produced a guide, *Copyright in Education*, which is highly recommended. For details contact the NCET.

The Computer Misuse Act

The Computer Misuse Act (1990) gives legal powers to stop 'hacking' (i.e. gaining access to computer systems for various mischievous and/or criminal purposes). The act recognises a number of new offences:

- A person knowingly causes a computer to perform any function with intent to secure unauthorised access to any program or data held in a computer.
- A person knowingly, and without authority, modifies the contents of any computer in order to impair its operation or hinder access to any program or data, or impair the operation of any program or the reliability of any data.

To prove an offence, it is necessary to demonstrate that the person who accessed the computer knew they were not authorised. The simplest means of doing this is to use passwords to control access.

Note that the first section can be applied to any computer user, not just hackers. Under this act, the copying of any computer data where that copying has not been authorised could be considered an offence. Moves are currently afoot to revise this act to increase the powers it grants to prosecute in cases of unauthorised access.

Data Protection Act 1984

This Act came out of very real concerns about the quantity of data being held on each individual person and that person's right to see what is being said about them. This section will deal with some of the obligations of senior managers in schools under the Act, but is not a step-by-step guide on how to register. The relevance of this Act can be tackled under four headings:

- The scope of the Act
- The principles of the Act
- Security of data
- Categories of sensitive data

The scope of the Act

Fundamentally, the Act demands that you assess exactly what personal data your school is gathering on computers, how it is stored and to whom you will make the data available. You will also need to assess whether you are acting as a 'Computer Bureau' (more will be said on this term later).

To be covered by the Act, personal data must fulfil two criteria:

- It must be held on computer.
- It must be about an individual person (a data subject) who can be identified and who is alive.

The 'data user' must register under the terms of the Act, and this data user is defined as the person or organisation or company who controls the contents and use of a collection of Personal data. The data user is NOT an employee. To work out who is the data user in a maintained school (not opted out) you need to look at all the functions which mean that data is stored. Then you have to find out who is legally responsible for the function and make sure that person or body is registered. Thus if a head teacher is holding data as an employee of the LEA then the LEA must register but if the head is storing data to discharge a legal duty then the head must register. Some examples will show how difficult this can be:

LEA	Staff records
	Contractors' records held in school
Governors	Curricular records
	Exam entries
Head	Annual reports to parents on pupils' achievements
	Results made under National Curriculum assessment arrangements.

If you are providing a facility for others (such as a PTA) to process a different set of data then you must register as a computer bureau. Usually it is the governing body who would register as a Bureau. The user of that data must register.

The principles of the Act

Personal data shall:

- Be obtained and processed fairly and lawfully. (Did the supplier of the data know what it would be used for?)
- Be held only for the lawful purposes described in the register entry. (The register entry must be kept up to date.)
- Be used only for those purposes and only disclosed to those people described in the register entry. (The purpose of the Act is NOT to keep the data secret but to make sure that its uses are known.)
- Be adequate, relevant and not excessive in relation to the purpose for which they are held. (Schools must decide carefully what is the minimum amount of data needed to perform a certain task. They are not to store data in case it might one day become useful.)
- Be accurate and, where necessary, kept up to date. (If this issue causes a problem, the Registrar will want to assess a number of factors: have reasonable steps been taken to ensure that data IS accurate? how much distress might be caused to the data subject by its inaccuracy? how quickly have errors been corrected?)
- Be held no longer than is necessary for the registered purpose. (This can be difficult for a school where data can be required for several years after pupils have left.)
- An individual shall be informed if data is being held, given access to that data, have the data corrected if it is wrong. (This is the heart of the whole Act: the individual has the right to know and correct!)
- Be surrounded by proper security. (This leads on the last heading: security of data.)

Security of Data

To fulfil the terms of the Act, it is strongly recommended by the Registrar that the following guidelines are followed:

Staff

- There must be a member of staff responsible for security procedures.
- Guidelines must be issued to other staff accessing data.
- Managers should be sure of the reliability of staff.

Privacy

- Equipment must be sited where it is not vulnerable to vandalism and where access can be restricted to authorised personnel.

- Screens and printers should be hidden from public view.
- Storage media (i.e. disks, tapes) should be locked away.
- Secure procedures for distribution of printed output should be set up.

Access

- Passwords should be used to restrict access to data.
- Password changes should be enforced and number of access attempts limited.
- Audit trails of access should be generated.
- Obsolete data must be deleted.

Sensitive Data

There are four categories of especially sensitive data which may be subject to subsequent legislation. No such legislation has appeared as yet, but it is as well to be aware that it may happen in the future. The categories are:

- racial origin
- political opinions or religious or other beliefs
- physical or mental health or sexual life
- criminal convictions.

Clearly there may be situations in which some of this data will be stored in a school, but it should always be the subject of special concern.

Siobhan Wharton works for Research Machines plc and may be contacted at New Mill House, 183 Milton Park, Abingdon, Oxon OX14 4SE.

CHAPTER EIGHT

Using IT for Staff Training

Jim Donnelly

There is a much greater awareness in schools of the need for training both teaching and non-teaching staff than there was even a decade ago. This has been partly due to the success of TVEI in raising the issue and the gradual devolution of training resources to schools (under GRIST, then LEATGS and now GEST). Appraisal has also played a part in raising school awareness of the need for training, which has led to many schools becoming involved in the Investors In People initiative of the Department of Employment. This has been given a further impetus with the recent changes in initial teacher training which put more emphasis on the school input.

The increasing interest in staff training has led many schools to consider how they might use IT to deliver this training. It is worth noting here that this interest in the use of IT for training does not only apply to its use for training staff to use IT but also to the delivery of training in response to the identification of needs covering a whole range of topics.

There are of course many different ways in which such training can be delivered. This chapter is concerned only with examples where the use of IT can help but at this point it should be made clear that the technology will only provide part of the answer.

Laservision

One particular technology which schools are beginning to use is Laservision. Its most common use to date has been in the area of staff training by businesses, including such diverse firms as Girobank and B&Q. It has not been used to any great extent in schools until quite recently.

Major factors inhibiting the use of this particular technology in education have been the cost of hardware and both the cost and lack of availability of software. When videodisc players cost £10,000 and discs cost typically over £1000 each, their purchase was clearly not viable for the average secondary school. It was also not viable for developers to produce discs for a non-existent educational market.

However, four factors are now coming together which make the use of laservision more than a remote possibility in schools. These are:

- It is now possible to purchase a videodisc player for under £3,000.
- Some school-specific software is becoming available at a cost which is more realistic for schools (typically £300-500). This has mainly been produced in Northern Ireland and Scotland.
- Discs are being developed for use in the curriculum, most notably the DFE-funded Mathematics discs and the recent initiative (managed by NCET) to trial existing discs in other areas of the curriculum. This means that the technology does not have to be used only for staff training.
- The Local Management of Schools (LMS) - and the consequently greater influence of business people on governing bodies - has changed the culture of schools and has made some of them at least more likely to be interested in buying technology which until now has been considered too expensive.

There is already some experience of the use of video in training both qualified and student teachers. There are two strands to this:

- Using pre-recorded video programmes on particular topics (e.g. managing meetings) or in specific subject areas (e.g. assessing oral work in English).
- Using video to record lessons and then to view them critically. This is not unknown in teacher training and will become more common in schools as a way of gathering useful evidence for the professional appraisal scheme.

Video is now relatively common (most schools have at least one video-recorder and video-camera) and blank tapes are very cheap. There is a dearth of pre-recorded training material of high quality at an affordable price for use in schools, but it can now only be a matter of time before such material reaches the market.

Even when that does happen, however, it is clear that there will a need for the particular strengths of Laservision.

The unique value of Laservision

A major difference between tape-based video and laser-disc video is that on the first the sound and pictures are presented on the same piece of tape while on the latter the pictures are quite separate from any instructional package. A second difference is that the latter uses digital technology.

There are four particular strengths following from these which mean that Laservision has a unique place in training.

1. The image quality is superb and it does not noticeably diminish with use.

2. It is easy to move quickly between one scene and another, to repeat a sequence and so on. (The best analogy is between music recorded on cassette, where it is very difficult to repeat tracks or even to find them in the first place, and music recorded on compact disc, which can be used much more flexibly.)

3. While the images on the videodisc cannot be easily changed, the sequence in which they are shown can be and the instruction can be varied. (This is because the disc contains the images while the computer contains all the instructions, both to the viewer and the disc.)

4. It is possible to build in a 'notepad', allowing it to be used as a form of distance learning. (More will be said about this later.)

If, as is suggested, interactive video has a unique role in training teachers, in what ways could it be used? There are two dimensions to the flexibility of Laservision:

• it can be used as a form of distance learning.
• the actual material can be manipulated, at high-speed.

As with any form of distance learning, the possibility is opened up of the material being used by one person (or a group) working independently. It can also be used by an instructor in the normal didactic way. The school's training manager can view sequences with a group of staff, followed by discussion, or they can view it on their own.

The manipulation of material at high speed allows both the tailoring of the instruction to suit the particular audience and also the use of 'What if...' scenarios. The latter means that teachers can be given a situation (e.g. a pupil misbehaving in class) with several possible ways of dealing with it. Each choice can be pursued and the (dis)advantages highlighted. There is then the choice of suggesting an ideal way of dealing with the situation or not, depending on the decision of the software writer.

The use of a 'notepad' adds a further dimension to the use of Laservision. This allows the training manager to write questions to the teacher who can work on the material at a different time and type in a reply, thus opening up a dialogue. This dialogue can be printed out and then used toward accreditation where such arrangements have been made.

As schools become more involved in teacher training there is a need for cost-effective but authoritative materials. Laservision is a particularly powerful way of providing these. Some specific uses of the technology for training teachers are:

- Provision of sequences from lessons, which can then be used to highlight good practice. Choices are then offered of different ways of dealing with incidents with possible consequences.
- Examples of incidents outside classrooms, which are often the most problematical for any teacher.
- Materials which highlight methods of teaching specific subjects.
- Different theories of education (e.g. 'potter and clay', 'mug and jug') juxtaposed, for comparison and contrast.
- Staff interactions, highlighting issues such as professionalism, responsibility to colleagues, and so on.
- Materials on the psychology of learning, motivation, and so on.
- Provision to write responses, including essays, to particular questions on chosen sequences.
- Examples from other countries of their approaches to primary or secondary education.

Given a suitable library of discs, very effective training - both in terms of quality and cost - can be carried out in schools by using this technology. At present discs are available on general management issues and on appraisal. More are being developed.

CDI

The compact disc which is used for home music and for CD-ROM is also used as the software for a system known as CDI. This has the potential to get into schools more quickly than Laservision, since it works from a CDI player (basically a black box which looks a bit like a cross between a video recorder and a satellite receiver) and plays through a standard television. The player costs a few hundred pounds, usually with some free discs, and some Laservision titles are being put onto CDI.

The advantages of the system are broadly the same as those for Laservision, although notepad facilities are not available. The cheaper cost of the hardware may well lead to schools being more disposed to using this technology, particularly since there are also discs available for curriculum use.

There is an increasing amount of school management training software available for CDI, with much of this being produced in Scotland. Many schools would find it cost-effective to have one player since off-site INSET or bringing in an outside speaker may be more expensive. Art teachers have found some very useful software and find CDI easy to use, largely because it plugs straight into an ordinary television set.

Desktop conferencing

This technology is fairly robust but is not yet used extensively in schools. The components of the system are two computers, with appropriate cards installed, and two ISDN boxes. An ISDN box (installed by BT and then subject to a quarterly rental charge) is essentially a double telephone link.

An example of how a project at Exeter University is using it will give some indication of its potential. The University is connected to a number of schools in South West England. A senior teacher in one of the schools has identified the need for regular training in the use of IT, particularly for word processing. However, the cost of going out of school for a half day each week is not one he is prepared to contemplate. He would be happier with a regular session of, say, half an hour every week at a time which suits him. Desktop conferencing allows him to have this. When he connects to the trainer in Exeter they can both speak to each other using a hands-free telephone. The other telephone line connects their computers, which allows the trainer to see what the teacher is doing on his computer and to suggest things he needs to do differently. It's like explaining something over the telephone without having to wave your arms about!

The technology can also be used for pupil learning and therefore the costs of the hardware and the line rental are shared across the training and the school capitation budgets.

A step up from desktop conferencing is video conferencing. This has been used for some time in industry, particularly by multi-nationals. Your computer has a small camera fixed onto the monitor which allows the person at the other end to see you during the conversation. More than two computers can be joined in this way. In itself, this may not attract too many people - the other person will also be able to see if you are signing letters or doing something else while you are supposedly giving them your undivided attention! However, it does allow you to show things and to demonstrate ideas visually as well as verbally.

Some work is also being done on the use of video-conferencing for pupils in isolated communities, and for pupils who are particularly gifted and would benefit from contact with experts in other institutions. Like many other things, using the technology for both management training and curriculum work can make it more cost-effective.

CHAPTER NINE

Purchasing IT Hardware and Software

David Keenliside

S chools face particular problems when investing in information technology since the rate of change is so rapid. IT is impossible to ignore since its importance is obvious whether in supporting the curriculum or in management decision-making. It is therefore vital that head teachers approach the purchase of both hardware and software in a strategic way in order to ensure that they decide on the most effective information technology solution for their needs.

Obviously all head teachers will need to make their decisions based on the particular circumstances of their own schools. This guidance is therefore restricted to a more general approach.

What is important is to avoid a piecemeal approach to procurement. This chapter will draw heavily on the NCET document, *Investing in IT,* free copies of which are still available. The purchasing process is a complex interaction of educational, technical, financial and management issues and requires the active involvement of several groups in the school. The timing of purchases is likely to have to fit in with the agreed cycle of review, and educational coherence must dominate the whole process. The whole-school IT policy - which is part of the School Development Plan - should include reference to the school's purchasing strategy. In this way a strategy for purchasing can be defined. The stages making up this strategy can be summarised as follows:

- Clarify your needs
- Choose software and hardware
- Formulate your plan
- Consider the financial options

58

- Write your purchasing strategy and incorporate it in your school development plan.

Remember that you may well find it both helpful and cost effective (particularly in the case of major purchases) to obtain independent professional advice. Bear in mind that there is a further cost associated with making decisions (staff involvement and time, for example, as well as any external advice) which has to be balanced against the size and importance of the investment proposed.

Clarifying your needs

Start by conducting an audit of the present situation. For curriculum uses, this will involve considering:

- Where in the curriculum, and at what key stages, your pupils gain IT experience and capability, directly and indirectly.
- Whether all pupils are gaining an appropriate variety of experiences.
- What resources are being used and how effectively they are being used.
- The staff involved and their levels of IT skills, confidence and experience.
- The teaching styles used.
- The place of IT within the School Development Plan and the cycle of review.

A similar audit can be conducted for management and administration uses. Clarify the position towards which you are working, as identified in the School Development Plan, because the decisions you make will need to be consistent with it. Look for ways in which a common operating system and hardware, together with a standard set of software, can strengthen coherence across the school, but be aware that some educational applications benefit from specialist systems. Identify the educational and technical training needs of the members of staff who will be involved. If changes in teaching styles are proposed, consider:

- the phasing of such groups (in certain departments, for example or for certain age groups)
- the support needed both during the changes and thereafter
- who could provide such support internally and externally - an IT Centre, for example.

Choosing software and hardware

An appropriate combination of hardware, software and associated teaching materials is vital if requirements are to be met.

Consider what software is required to meet the needs which you have identified. Check that these key issues have been addressed:
• compatibility with both the existing hardware and software
• maintenance costs and security of long-term support
• any needs for specific or general training for staff and students.

If new or upgraded software is proposed, look for opportunities to increase its value in use; check whether it can enhance or be enhanced by linkage with other software. Ensure that all costs are considered, including annual subscriptions and telephone charges for electronic communications, and check that the licensing arrangements for any packages purchased are suitable for your needs. Buying a single package will normally only allow its use on one machine, so a site licence or a network licence may be more appropriate (see also Chapter 7). Sometimes class or school packs of software can also be purchased for multiple stand-alone machines on one site.

Try to arrange for the IT co-ordinator or another appropriate member of staff to evaluate the software prior to purchase by, for example:
• seeing the software in action in a school environment
• talking to existing users
• asking for a demonstration at a local IT or teachers' centre, at an exhibition or from the supplier.

When selecting hardware it is worth seeking advice on current recommended specifications from the equipment manufacturers and your local IT centre. Before a major purchase, ensure that your IT co-ordinator or another appropriate member of staff sees the equipment in action in a school environment, with an opportunity to talk with the users. Alternatively, you may be able to assess the suitability of different systems at exhibitions, through reading manufacturers' literature and demonstrations at teachers' and local IT centres, at local dealers, in published reviews, if supplied on approval.

Assess the specification of new equipment proposed against three criteria:

1. A minimum specification needed to meet the school's immediate requirements; this will usually be the cheapest option, but may limit future expansion.

2. A modest specification which exceeds the minimum and will allow future expansion and upgrading without the need for expensive modifications. Think about the main processor, the capacity of the hard disc and resolution or colour of display. It will be easy to add memory, a network card, or a mouse or other input device.

3. A maximum specification which can meet any needs you envisage at the moment. This is likely to be expensive unless you can predict future needs accurately.

Remember to consider upgrading your present system. This may be more cost effective than buying a new system. You will need to consider the reliability of your system once upgraded and how many years of useful life it will be reasonable to expect. Bear in mind also that in real terms, computer hardware is becoming more affordable.

Whether you want to upgrade your existing hardware or buy new, bear in mind the following factors:
• compatibility with existing software
• ability to run new, more modern software
• ability to connect with a network or increase its efficiency
• the provision of additional facilities such as sound
• printing or access to CD-ROM
• flexibility of deployment
• familiarity of staff and pupils with existing software.

If you decide to replace your old system, its usefulness may not end there; it could be released for other uses, provided that it is still reliable enough and maintenance is not too difficult or expensive.

When buying a new system, assess the arguments for and against networking. This is an issue which still creates debate within education, although the trend elsewhere is now clearly towards using networks. A summary of the main factors to be considered is given in *Investing in IT.*

Also consider whether any alterations will be needed to existing accommodation (such as room partitions, installation of power supplies and/or network cables) and obtain a realistic estimate of the ongoing cost of consumables where appropriate: for example, for printers this will be toner or ink cartridges/ribbons.

If the purchase of equipment is just for management and administration purposes, additional points which you should bear in mind include:

- looking for any essential compatibility with LEA systems, other schools, and with Examination Boards
- security arrangements both for the physical equipment and for data
- identifying those members of staff who will need to use both the curriculum and the administration systems and assessing any personal or technical training needs.

If you are introducing a new system, staff training will be the critical factor in the timescale for implementation. Do not forget security issues. It is no use having well-thought out plans for hardware and software if it is all stolen after installation.

Formulating a plan

Once you have drawn up a specification of hardware and software requirements and considered the option of networking, a range of additional factors will need consideration:

- compatibility between software, hardware and peripherals
- initial training and ongoing support
- maintenance requirements
- legal issues and questions of copyright
- data protection
- health and safety requirements.

Compatibility

This includes the ways in which free-standing software interacts with the operating system and with different items of hardware. Problems that do arise are usually more critical when between items of hardware (network and peripherals such as CD-ROM drives, for example) than between individual programs.

Look for ways in which a common operating system combined with a standard set of software, can help to facilitate coherence across the school. Lack of compatibility between pieces of software and hardware, and between computers and peripherals such as printers, inevitably means a lack of flexibility in their use.

Software

If software is being upgraded, ensure that existing files (for example, data about pupils' examination entries or examination work) will run easily and effectively on the new system. An example would be when a new library management system is being installed.

Hardware

Similarly, if hardware is being upgraded, ensure that important existing uses will run easily and effectively on the new system. If you are purchasing equipment from different manufacturers, make certain that the detailed specifications in the tenders state explicitly who will be responsible for installation, operation, and maintenance and repairs. This is absolutely crucial if the equipment is to be linked on the same network. You will also need to assess the costs and effectiveness of separate maintenance agreements (as opposed to an overall contract), if there are several different makes and types of equipment in use.

Portables

If you already have portable computers, or are thinking of buying portables, consider the issues involved when they are used in conjunction with the 'mainstream' computers or a network, for example:

• ease and speed of transfer of files
• access to and links with printers
• anti-virus controls.

An important point about portables is that they extend practice, for example when they are used on field trips. It can also make sense to provide certain low cost portables which may be appropriate for your needs. Do you really need an expensive desktop or could you use a less expensive portable which enables pupils to learn basic skills? A range of NCET publications about portable computers is available from NCET sales.

Compatibility beyond school

Find out what computer systems are used by other organisations with which you may wish to exchange data, for example other schools, the LEA or examination bodies. You may find that this can be done through 'electronic data interchange', a form of electronic communication.

Training and ongoing support

It is essential to invest in training and ongoing support whenever a major investment is made in new IT hardware and/or software. The training may be to develop specific skills using a few software packages, and it may include teaching strategies and resource materials to support IT in the National Curriculum. The training requirements will include:

- sharing the vision with staff colleagues about the potential of the new purchase(s)
- detailed training for those who will be using the resources
- technical training for the staff who will be responsible for providing first-line support
- arranging ongoing support, including new staff.

Maintenance

This can be provided by a range of agencies including:

- school-based staff (including technicians)
- LEA support services
- local dealers and IT Centres
- manufacturers.
- specialist maintenance companies, who sometimes offer insurance-linked post-warranty contracts; these may be local, or national organisations with local agents.

Warranty

Identify those items which are covered by warranty agreements, and those covered by maintenance contracts. On-site, rapid repair is important for 'critical' parts of the system such as network servers. Consider also the availability of replacement equipment and maintain accurate records of what IT resources are installed. If different agencies are to be responsible for maintaining different parts of a complex system such as a computer network, insist that the responsibilities of each agency are clearly defined.

Making back-ups

Ensure that the IT co-ordinator operates effective regular procedures to back up systems so that data which has been accidentally deleted can be restored quickly and easily. This is especially the case for networks where it is useful to have a system which can be set to automatically back up, at regular intervals.

Regular, effective checks and rigorous controls on computer viruses are also an essential part of the maintenance programme. This is normally the responsibility of the IT co-ordinator.

It is vital to have guidance on legal issues including copyright, data protection and health and safety issues. Full details of the relevant laws and regulations must be obtained from the authorities such as the Health and Safety Executive and the Data Protection Agency (see also Chapter 7).

Financial issues

Although computer costs have fallen in recent years, it is unwise to delay decisions about the purchase of IT equipment to the point that pupils and staff are placed at major educational or professional disadvantage. All IT resources have a finite useful life. The factors which will decide when to 'write off' such items are:

• when there is educational disadvantage in further use
• when the maintenance costs (in terms of finance and staff time) become too great.

Schools have a number of options including purchasing and finance leases and rental agreements (ensure that the latter meet LEA or other public service requirements). Remember that schools need to develop a policy for using their older computers which may be dated, but are still perfectly functional in curriculum terms.

Write your purchasing strategy

Having considered all these issues you should now be in a position to decide on the purchasing strategy that would be of most benefit to your own institution. Finally, remember to incorporate this within the School Development Plan so that you are in a position to ensure that it supports the priorities that have been identified for your school.

David Keenliside is a Programme Manager at the National Council for Educational Technology.

CHAPTER TEN

IT and
Special Needs

Sally McKeown

nformation technology is not a panacea. Used badly, it simply replaces boring paper-based exercises with boring computer tasks. However, when used skilfully, it can make for more effective teaching and learning; it can teach us about the abilities of the children and it can help young people leave full-time education better able to make their own way in the world.

A pupil with special needs does not necessarily need a special solution. In fact, many of the resources you need are already in your schools. Often all that is needed is an adaptation such as using a speech chip or an overlay keyboard with a standard package. The following examples show what IT has to offer with examples of what it has done for pupils of different ages.

Developing literacy

Dean dare not write because the spelling might be wrong. A word processor with a concept keyboard overlay enables him to write without asking for words. He can get used to putting in words he is not sure about because they can be changed later when he has finished his story.

A simple word processor program offers far more than a typewriting facility. A whole group may gather round a large-print display on the computer screen, discussing wording and content. An individual child, hesitant at committing words to paper with pen or pencil, is freed from the worry and frustration of making mistakes. The user of the word processor is assured of a presentable result, which may be in large print for display purposes.

The word processor may actively support the user by providing a personalised bank of words to be keyed in at a single touch from an overlay keyboard, or by offering a dictionary and/or a check on spelling. Some word processors provide pictures or speech to stimulate writing. Other programs support the development of writing skills by offering a framework for creative writing or by inviting the user to create a story by accepting or rejecting the offerings of the computer program. Another approach is to offer an exciting format such as a newspaper page layout complete with headlines.

The Talking Computer project in Somerset uses Archimedes computers which can exploit speech to support reading and spelling. The children made startling improvements in a matter of weeks. Their reading age increased by up to 37 months, the average being by 10.6 months; spelling ages improved by up to 12 months and there were significant improvements in concentration, short term memory and self-esteem. The children had only received 20 minutes tuition a day for 4 weeks and the progress was maintained at follow-up testing 10 weeks and 6 months later.

Speech is a useful tool, especially when used in conjunction with other strategies as in Richard's case:

Richard has been using the program Full Phase for his class project about the Tudors. He is writing in blue text on a yellow background because he finds that combination easier to read for long periods. His teacher has created a word bank of common words that he struggles to write. He copy types these as a way of fixing the spellings in his mind. He has another list of words and phrases for the Tudors including Elizabeth, Sir Francis Drake, divorced, beheaded, survived. He inserts these by clicking on them because they are not words he needs to be able to spell at this stage but they are words he needs to access for this project. If he cannot decode any of the words, he can listen to them. All his writing is using a multisensory approach: he is looking at the words in the word bank, touching the letters on the keyboard, seeing the words take shape on the screen and hearing what he has written.

If you are going to use speech, invest in some headphones. This will ensure that the pupil maintains privacy and that the rest of the class are not disturbed.

Fostering a more child-centred approach

IT can offer a way of presenting complex information in bite-sized chunks. Children are able to control the computer at a pace they determine. They take decisions about the outcomes and sometimes about the input to the computer. In addition a child may accept a negative response from the computer which would not be acceptable from a teacher. In this way, the experience becomes child-centred and child-controlled.

Adventure games are a good example. The best adventure games encourage the user to make and test predictions and to develop an investigative approach "what happens if I ...?" The games provide an opportunity to make mistakes without risking the red pen and as users correct their own mistakes they become much more self-reliant. Above all, the user learns by doing. Initially it might be by trial and error, then it might be by recalling the exact procedure they used last time and then it might be by thinking about strategies which have worked before in similar situations. In other words, they start to develop and test hypotheses.

Andrew has a history of disruptive behaviour, is nearly nine years old but has a reading age of 5.3. His mathematical ability is low but he is starting to grasp place value and addition of hundreds, tens and units and also subtraction without exchange.

Andrew used *Rescue: An Island Adventure*. The purpose of the game is to rescue an 'absent minded uncle' from a number of difficulties. To rescue Uncle from a mine shaft, Andrew had to collect the right length of rope from the friendly lighthouse keeper. The first time he did this, Andrew was in a hurry and collected the wrong length. He carried it all the way to the mine shaft and lowered it down but it did not reach. He sighed, walked out of the mine back to the lighthouse and this time took a lot more trouble to fetch the correct length.

Andrew enjoyed the fact that he could wander anywhere he wanted on the island. Although he found parts of it difficult, he was sufficiently motivated to keep going and to find ways of solving problems. Despite his previous behavioural problems, he was not frustrated when he collected the wrong length of rope but started again. Above all, it did wonders for his self-esteem because he was in control and could decide what to do next.

For learners who have problems following verbal explanations, or who struggle to record what they mean in an accurate and acceptable form, adventure games are very liberating. They offer opportunities for success which are not entirely dependent on notation or neat presentation. In addition, adventure games may provide a meaningful context for undertaking writing and maths activities. After they have got lost a few times, they realise that they need to record their findings systematically if they want to reach their goal so, for once, they have a valid reason for writing things down, rather than doing it just because they have been told to.

Using IT to give access to the curriculum.
IT can go some way towards removing the barrier to the curriculum that poor language skills create. Much of the vocabulary and content of a topic can be introduced to pupils before they use a package, thus enabling concepts to be absorbed and manipulated more easily.

Jan is in year 9 and finds it difficult to get information from printed text. She is particularly interested in Geography and wants to find out information about tourist attractions in Egypt for a project. Normally she would struggle to find the information in books. She uses Encarta, a multimedia encyclopaedia on CD ROM in the library. She types in 'E' in the index and finds the entries starting with these letters. She selects 'Egypt' which she can recognise even though she cannot spell it. When the entry comes up on the page, she copies it into Microsoft Word, and uses the speech option to have each sentence read out to her. This enables her to concentrate on the information and select the details she wants.

This CD ROM is not a special needs product. By using a speech facility, Jan is able to have access to the same information as anyone else. Many SEN learners remain locked into a dependent learning mode, where adults (teachers, assistants and parents) and often other children or students become essential. This, in the long term, saps confidence, damages self-image and limits learning.

Multimedia packages can bring together a picture or video clip with text and a spoken commentary. In fact you can have talking worksheets so that if you want to explain or expand some of the information, such as the reasons for using particular words, you can click on an area on the screen, record your voice into the computer, and then stop recording. The content on the screen remains the same but the messages can be different for different groups of students.

Sue Price of the Outreach Unit at Wolverley High School in Kidderminster feels that technology can make a significant contribution to teaching modern foreign languages:

"With the newer technologies, students can listen and practise their speaking skills and compare versions. They can practise vocabulary by labelling pictures or filling in a cloze passage on screen or searching through the text on a CD ROM. It can make reinforcement and learning more interesting so pupils use different techniques to learn vocabulary and to reinforce learning from another area."

Making the most of what you've got

These examples are all very well but what can you do if you've only got one computer for 30 children? How will this allow for differentiation? A first step might be to encourage and provide time for staff to use the word processor to make handouts. This will improve the pupils' skills and competence, it will allow them to learn by problem solving and it can provide differentiated worksheets for the class. Some might need additional information. Evidence has shown that when staff use the word processor for their own work they are more committed and better able to see ways of using IT with their pupils

IT doesn't need to be a computer. Some schools are making use of fax machines as a way of motivating reluctant writers. Because fax transmits so quickly, it is possible to establish a dialogue with other schools. Some small rural schools are linking up with others and writing chain letters while others are being more ambitious and linking up to schools in France and Germany to exchange information, including pictures and maps.

But lower tech solutions can be just as effective. Do not despise the tape recorder and camera. Differentiation can be at a simple level. Take the example of Don who has difficulties in producing any sort of creative writing. Why not let him draft it on tape?

Sometimes if a pupil is only producing a few lines of illegible text it is difficult to tell whether the major stumbling block is in the composing or the writing. The taped story can be transcribed by the child at a later time or at home by the parents or by a teacher or classroom assistant. The child can then refine the draft and make alterations. For once, he is involved in composing and creating and thinking like a writer instead of always struggling with the mechanics of putting text on paper.

Find out what programs you've got and think about how they could be used. Spreadsheets are useful not just for number work but also for making grids and tables and for display work. The small cells do not take lengthy scripts and may motivate reluctant writers

Deciding what to buy

Too often purchasing consists of a series of ad hoc decisions. If you have already undertaken an audit of resources and skills within the school, then it is easier to identify items of software and hardware which will complement and extend existing provision. When buying new equipment it is important to decide when the SEN pupils need access and exactly what they need access to.

Do they really need a portable computer or just a word processor? Do they need access to a spell checker and if so does this need to be part of a word processor package or would a SpellMaster serve their purposes better? If they really need access to a computer for all their subjects, what about homework? Should they take their machine home? Is the portable compatible with the desktop machines in the school?

Training and support for staff is essential if the SEN pupils are to receive adequate support. The technology is of little use if staff and pupils struggle to use it or if it is seen as a bolt-on extra to an already overloaded curriculum. It should be a tool to make life easier. Many schools have overlay keyboards which can be of enormous benefit to a wide range of pupils and yet they are an underused resource because staff do not have the time to devise materials or work with other staff to discover the most effective ways of using them with their learners. Time put aside for training is well worth the initial cost.

When planning an IT policy, it is always wise to project forward and try to keep abreast of new developments; both the technology and our awareness of what it can do for individuals is rapidly changing.

Wouldn't it be nice if...

In the future, more schools will be using class sets of laptops and this will again change the way that we view technology and the ways in which we use it. There is a danger that, without training, many staff will use them just as glorified typewriters. Compare these two schools:

In school A, while the rest of the class were doing some really imaginative work on the Victorians, a certain number were called out to finish copy typing their previous work - a story about a robbery - on the portables. In fact the IT was obviously seen by the teacher as an extra or alternative activity, not as a part of her normal lesson.

But in school B, the teacher used the machines as part of a strategy to provide differentiated approaches to story writing.

In school B the class had 10 Archimedes Pocket Books and were using them to create Partner stories. They worked in pairs, drafting and redrafting stories. Eventually there would be 10 photocopies of each story - 2 for the library, 2 for the class set, 2 for each child to take home and one each for their record of work folder.

It was interesting to see the children making decisions about the technology. Some chose to print out from the portables and cut and paste their stories with hand drawn pictures; others transferred their stories to a desktop machine and incorporated drawings done on a paint package before printing.

The children were at ease with the technology and there were many examples of their word processing in the classroom. They used the spell checker facility very confidently and the teacher focused on the content and phrasing of their work, not on the technology. There are plans for a parallel class to use the portables next term for database work which will be the basis of a penpal scheme with a school in another part of the country.

Technology is advancing rapidly and coming down in price. These are the key areas you should keep an eye on:

Interactive Video

This allows film and photograph sequences to be used with high quality sound to present material which is more real and life-like compared to the 'cartoon' images of traditional software. It has the potential to make a significant impact on all forms of simulations and role play.

CD ROMs

This form of data storage gives the student access to massive amounts of information. This information could be in the form of text, images, sound, moving video and combinations of all these media.

Photo CD

This is a way of recording images onto a CD. Playback is via a CDI player, a domestic photo CD player or via the CD ROM drive on a computer.

Scanners/video camera/still video/digitisers

It is relatively easy to capture images from a wide variety of sources including pre-recorded and 'live' video tape. This will have a major impact on recording and self profiling as 'real life' scenarios can simply be transferred to paper and printed out.

Laser Printers

These high quality printers are becoming more accessible to schools as prices become more affordable. This will enhance the quality of documents such as Records of Personal Achievement, Curricula Vitae and Profiles.

Internet

This is a vehicle for access to world-wide information since users can talk to people on the opposite side of the world and also can delve into databases developed by multi-national corporations. For example, some schools have started to download satellite photographs and superb graphics of spacecraft from the NASA database.

This final example from Hertfordshire shows how the newer technologies can enhance the learning process:

An opportunity for pupils to use interactive video based on laser discs was provided by equipment loaned by the Hertfordshire Schools Road Safety Service. This was used by pupils to support a course in cycling proficiency. This medium clearly illustrated its capacity to hold pupils' attention and engage them in the process of learning, pupils responded particularly well to the high quality of the sound and vision and identified with the realism of the scenarios it presented.

Sally McKeown is a Senior Programme Officer at the National Council for Educational Technology.

CHAPTER ELEVEN

Advising Parents about Computers

Jenny Brown

"My child wants a computer, have you got any suggestions?" Most schools have found themselves in this position and are likely to have their advice increasingly sought as retailers have launched a marketing attack on parents, encouraging them to buy technology for the home - computer games, personal computers, printers.

The UK video games industry turned over in excess of £700 million last year, which is proof enough that parents are prepared to spend money on technology. Eight out of ten children aged between 11 and 14 now play video games and six out of ten have their own games machine.

As these machines become more sophisticated, children will be able to do more than just play games at home. They will be able to access a wide range of information on CD-ROM and link via communications technology to computer networks around the world. Manufacturers and retailers are aware of this and are beginning to move in on the home market with some determination. Schools will be asked for advice and may well be able to influence what is bought so that it can complement the computer resources held in school. This chapter is to help schools respond sensibly to parents' requests for advice.

How would you decide on a family car?

Buying a computer for the home is a bit like buying a family car: you need to list all the things you would like it to be able to do and then match these against what you can afford to pay. Although a desktop computer with a printer, colour monitor, a multimedia facility and a range of software will probably cost more than £1000 it is possible to buy a pocket-sized word processor that will do a great deal to help a child at school for about £100. Parents need to ask a number of questions before they set out to buy:

- Who will use the computer? Will it be specifically for the children or will it be used to write business letters or to produce newsletters for a club or society for example?

- What will they want to do? Children may think they only want to play games but it would help their school work if they could use a word processor and spreadsheet at home.

- Do we need to have a printer? It is very frustrating not to be able to print what you have written so it is pretty essential; and, of course, the better the quality of the printer the better the work looks.

- Do we need to buy the same computer as the children use at school? Not necessarily, but it could be useful to ensure that discs used in school could be taken home to finish work.

There are some suppliers who offer leasing or rental facilities for computers and it might be useful to make enquiries in your own area so that you can provide parents with information. Parents might not realise that they could rent a computer on a similar basis as they do the TV or video recorder.

Collective purchase

A school might want to encourage parents to buy a particular portable computer, which is compatible with the desktop machines used in school. In this case, it might be possible to set up special purchasing deals with a supplier. This could include support for expenses such as batteries, discs and repairs. Parents might then group together to buy a colour printer (or other more expensive peripherals) that could be used by all the children. The school would have the advantage of more computers in the classroom and the parents would have bought something appropriate and useful.

Parents making individual purchases could be advised to look at one or two of the computer shopping magazines such as *Computer Shopper* or *Computer Buyer* to compare prices. These offer mail-order services which mean that wherever you live you can take advantage of a good deal. It is important to stress to parents the value of extended warranties and the need for good service agreements.

Equality of access
There will always be children whose parents will not be able to provide a computer at home and schools need to develop strategies to support them, perhaps by providing a number of machines which could be borrowed for home use or by encouraging the local library to make some available after school hours.

Parents of girls may need more encouragement to provide a computer for them at home. Almost twice as many boys as girls use a computer at home and a recent study found that boys are thirteen times more likely to have a computer bought for them than girls. Studies also show that girls use computers more effectively - they like to work for a real purpose and are more likely to be word processing than playing games.

Video games
Although teachers can read a lot of evidence about the value of computers to learning, parents reading the popular press might not get the same positive impression.

There has been a great deal of discussion in the media about the possible adverse effects of playing video games and parents may be looking to the school for reassurance. Video games are the most popular toys around, they are fun and children can spend hours playing them.

The concerns fall into three groups:
Medical hazards
It had been suggested that playing video games could induce epileptic fits but research has shown that it is only photosensitive epilepsy which is triggered by the type of flickering light found in video games. Once diagnosed, children can still play so long as they wear an eye patch over one eye. Parents can get more advice from the British Epilepsy Association helpline (01345 089599). Other health hazards attributed to video game playing are migraine headaches and eyesight problems. Both these conditions seem to improve when the time spent playing games is limited.

Violent content

The content of many video games is violent and this is worrying because it suggests to children that violence is the only way to solve problems. Some head teachers have reported that children role playing situations from the games often continue to behave aggressively in the playground or classroom. Some games show female or ethnic minority characters in submissive or inferior roles and these ideas are at odds with the ideas of equal opportunities being promoted in our schools. Many parents just don't know what is in the games their children are playing; they need to become more aware and to monitor the games their children buy or swap at school.

Addictive playing

Some children become obsessive about playing video games, parents should make sure that video game playing is just one of many activities: sport, clubs, reading and television, for example can all contribute to a balanced recreational diet.

Computer pornography

Just as it exists in books, magazines and films it is possible to produce pornography on a computer. Material held on a disc can be easily copied and sold or given away in the playground. The rapid growth in the use of the Internet (a worldwide network of computers linked by telecommunications) has increased concern about children getting access to unacceptable material.

This technology opens up a world of often free information sources to schools and enables children to tap into world-wide expertise - it would be a shame to lose all this because we cannot manage the pornography problem. Parents and teachers are our first line of defence in this; they should make sure they know what is being viewed on home and school computers and be ready to discuss with children why pornography is unacceptable.

What can schools do to involve parents?

Some schools run courses for parents which help them gain an accredited skill whilst widening their understanding of what their children are doing. Others may decide to issue general guidelines to parents in the form of a letter or news sheet. If this is done it might be useful to include the following advice:

- Bring the computer into the family areas of your home.
- Take an interest in what your children are doing with the computer; learn to use it yourself. The multimedia revolution will change the nature of learning and your children will need your support.
- If you have a modem manage its use - you could run up large telephone bills if you don't!
- Keep your credit cards under control!

The National Council for Educational Technology has produced a video games fact sheet, *Video Games, Advice for Parents*, which schools might find useful.

Jenny Brown is a Programme Manager with the National Council for Educational Technology.

Introduction

Considerable experience of the use of IT in the curriculum is being developed in schools. At present the situation is very patchy with considerable variation between schools, not only across the country but even at a local level. Much of this experience is shared through the informal networks which operate within the teaching profession, through subject and professional associations, and through exhibitions.

In this book some examples are given of uses in some subject areas. They are meant as examples of what can be done, not as *exemplars*. It will be some time yet before the use of IT will have reached the state of maturity where definitive guidance can be given for every teacher. The most important factor in how quickly expertise is shared is the enthusiasm of classroom teachers in using the technology in an innovative way. Schools which are using IT imaginatively are not necessarily those which have spent most money on equipment.

The publishers would like to hear of good practice for publication in the magazines *Managing Schools Today*, and *InteracTive*, and in future editions of this handbook.

CHAPTER TWELVE

Using CD-ROM in the Primary School

Maureen Quigley

When the staff and pupils at Ravensdale Junior and Infant School in Coventry took delivery of a new computer, they were one of nearly 5,000 lucky schools chosen by their Local Education Authority in 1994 to participate in a two-phase government initiative to introduce CD-ROM technology into primary schools.

The CD-ROM in Primary Schools initiative has been funded to the tune of £9.5m by the Department for Education and managed by The National Council for Educational Technology. As part of the initiative, schools received a multimedia workstation which consisted of a computer with a colour monitor, a CD-ROM drive, a set of external speakers, headphones and a bundle of CD-ROM discs. This 100% funded scheme meant that 4,966 primary schools in England are now discovering what multimedia can add to the learning process.

Selecting the CD-ROM titles to go with each of the machines in this project was a huge task that had to be completed in a short period of time. Suppliers and publishers of CD-ROMs were invited to submit suitable titles to be evaluated; NCET undertook to do the rest. Subsequently 454 CD-ROM discs arrived in Coventry submitted by 69 different suppliers.

A team of 40 people who not only had an understanding of multimedia but were also familiar with the requirements of National Curriculum at KS1 and KS2 was assembled, with representatives from primary schools, Local Education Authorities, Library and Information Services, professional and subject associations and HMI. Working in small groups of two or three, they reviewed all the discs.

Disc evaluation

A unifying set of common criteria was developed and the evaluation
team used these to ensure that a consistent assessment was made of
each title. First they had to score each disc on a scale from 1 to 5
against the following headings:

- Adequacy of content and coverage of the information on the disc
- Accuracy and currency of the information on the disc
- Appropriateness to the National Curriculum in England
- Appropriateness of the reading age to KS 1 and KS2 pupils
- Quality of the interface design and presentation
- Level of interactivity and indexing of the material
- Overall quality of the disc

They were then asked to write a review of the disc which referred to
the criteria listed above. The result was a set of 400-plus reviews which
are remarkably informative, as this extract from the review of *Microsoft
Art Gallery* shows. It highlights the aspects of content and coverage:

"This disc contains 2000 paintings from the National Gallery in
London. It is extensive, well presented and informative. As a KS1/2
resource it would be invaluable, but would require additional support
material for use by the non specialist (for example, starting points for
investigation, suggested activities). As well as looking at works of art,
artists, historical settings, it also has information on how and which
media have been used and explanations of specialist terminology."

Another example touches on the issue of currency and accuracy
of information:

"This is a world atlas on CD-ROM. The maps are very detailed.
However some inaccuracies were noted on the maps of London and
Greater London."

But the reviewers wanted to go beyond just recording the bare
facts about the discs. They wanted to include their impressions and
reactions to certain discs.

This is taken from the review of *Arthur's Teacher Trouble:*

"...This is the technical equivalent of a pop-up book, with its
emphasis on enjoyment...Overall, the package represents a fun reading experience for children of around 6 to 9 years of age."

Finally the evaluators were asked to recommend whether the disc
should be included in purchases for the initiative. This three-pronged

approach led to a thorough and measured evaluation being made across all the submitted titles.

If a title scored highly, got a good review, and was recommended for inclusion then it joined an 'A' stream of titles. These were then mapped against curriculum subjects and types of material to provide a range of titles for the schools. This resulted in a list of possible titles which was used to open negotiations with suppliers.

Apart from using this process to make a final selection of 34 titles for the bundles, all the evaluations done for the initiative have been published in a guidance document which contains 449 reviews, and comes complete with subject indexes, approximate prices, suppliers names and addresses, dates of publication, countries of origin and suitability for KS1 and KS2. Primary schools not involved can reap some benefits of this work by ordering the purchasers' guide, *CD-ROM Titles Review*, from NCET (please include a cheque for £8.50). Schools and Local Education Authorities often ask for information on discs that is free from commercial interests, rather than a list of what is available, and these reviews fall into that category.

Distribution

The NCET has specified, selected and tested all the equipment and CD-ROM discs being given to the schools, and is managing the complex task of delivery, set up and demonstration of the discs. Machines representing the most commonly found computer platforms in schools are included in the initiative: PC, Acorn A5000 and Apple. We were keen to ensure that each bundle contained a reference work in the form of an encyclopaedia, literary works, such as stories or poems, and specific curriculum support material covering a number of subjects including: history, geography, science, art and music. Each bundle contained discs suitable for both KS1 and KS2.

This strategy of providing hardware with a bundle of software, had several advantages. The volume of purchases meant that NCET was able to provide many more schools with high performance computers and CD-ROM discs than any single local initiative could afford to do; and the central selection of discs meant that schools start with a range of titles which offer a wide and balanced mix of material, with the opportunity to see which are most useful. Teachers are able to disseminate any locally developed support materials more widely and the experience of using and managing the learning associated with specific CD-ROM discs can be shared. The fact that all the discs schools have received were evaluated by a team of primary specialists, means that they will not have to spend money on unseen and untried resources which may not be suitable for classroom use.

Maureen Quigley is a Senior Programme Officer at the National Council for Educational Technology.

CHAPTER THIRTEEN

Using Multimedia in Mathematics

Jane Spilsbury

Pupils in schools across the country are running to maths lessons. Some can be found waiting on the school steps for the doors to open, just so that they can 'have a go' on a new computer system. What is going on? This chapter gives an example of one laservision purchase being used in schools to learn aspects of mathematics.

The cause of all this excitement is *The World of Number,* an interactive multimedia package which includes laserdiscs, computer software and printed support materials.

'Multimedia' is the mixture of text and graphics with motion and sound, including video, audio, animation and photographs. The system is interactive because it allows the pupil to control the images quickly and easily using a mouse, keyboard or even a barcode reader.

When maths teachers were asked what they thought of the materials, their reactions were very positive. They value the fact that the materials were designed to meet the needs of the National Curriculum; indeed, they were commissioned by the National Curriculum Council. They found the interactive nature of the materials very motivating. Pupils receive instant feedback on their answers. The materials present maths problems in a realistic way, providing a bridge between the conceptual and the concrete.

Pupils were even more enthusiastic, particularly those who had previously shown little or no interest in maths! Their favourite section was 'Who stole the Decimal Point?', where pupils are invited to solve the mystery of the missing decimal point by solving a series of maths problems hidden in rooms around 'Integer Hall'. The problems are very challenging. In other circumstances these particular pupils may never have attempted them, let alone volunteered to work through their lunch hour! Their fear of failure is removed because only the computer sees their answer. Even the teacher need not see it.

Although *The World of Number* has been trialled on interactive video (IV) systems, the secondary material is already available on CD-ROM and there are plans to transfer the primary material in the near future.

Of course, teachers faced the perennial problem of sharing one system between thirty pupils, but this was overcome in most cases by the nature of the activities. Some can be viewed and then solved away from the computer, others need to be solved on-screen.

But why have teachers made the effort this time to tackle the problems usually associated with the use of new technology in education? They have done so because the materials are subject specific and relevant to the National Curriculum. Teachers recognise that this is an opportunity too good to be missed.

Copies of the report *IV in Schools*, which gives further details of the project, are available from the National Council for Educational Technology, Milburn Hill Road Science Park, Coventry CV4 7JJ.

Jane Spilsbury is a Field Officer at the National Council for Educational Technology.

CHAPTER FOURTEEN

Using IT
in Science

Keith Hemsley

I T can underpin science lessons, making them challenging and fun. For example, a class were observing and testing a collection of sugars. They wrote about their observations using a word processor and used a graph drawing programme to display their investigations of the time each sugar took to dissolve in water. They found that caster sugar took 12 seconds to dissolve, brown sugar took 26 seconds, granulated sugar took 45 seconds and preserving sugar took 50 seconds. They concluded that these variations had something to do with the size and hardness of the granules. They were able to use IT to communicate their findings.

Using the computers which schools are now buying - ranging from PC compatibles to Research Machines' Window Box, Apple Macintosh computers and Acorn's Archimedes range - makes it much easier to move text and images between applications. In this case it was easy to combine text and a graph to produce a report of their activities.

Handling information

The same group of children also recorded their observations using Noticeboard, a simple card-file database, on their BBC Master computer (similar programs are available on other computers). This type of database records information using a few lines of text and up to four key words. The children had to think carefully about what words they used and what features, common to a number of sugars, were suitable as key words. Once they had entered observations on all their sugars they were able to search the database looking, for example, for all the sugars with a crystal structure.

The value of using this type of database comes from the close observation, classification skills and careful choice of language involved in the construction of the database. Such databases tend to have less than twenty records and have limited possibilities for searching for patterns in the data. However, there are much larger, pre-prepared data-files available for children to use as reference material in their science work. The popular database, *Key,* for example, has a number of science related data-files with not only a wealth of textual information but also many high quality images and diagrams.

With the increasing popularity of CD-ROM as a medium for storing and presenting vast amounts of data, it is likely that children will soon have very large databases of information available to them. Take, for example, Hutchinson's Encyclopaedia on CD-ROM; children are able to refer to over 27,000 articles, 2,500 illustrations and many sound recordings.

Resources available to help science teachers think about and develop their use of IT include *InteracTive,* a new magazine from Questions Publishing, *IT's Primarily Science* and *Primary Science Investigations with IT,* which are available free from the National Council for Educational Technology. For those who are considering buying CD-ROMs, NCET has prepared a comprehensive guide. *CD-ROM Titles Review 1995* comments on nearly 500 CD-ROMs and their relevance to National Curriculum subjects.

Keith Hemsley is a Senior Programme Officer at the National Council for Educational Technology.

CHAPTER FIFTEEN

Using IT
in Music

John Dempsey

Technology has changed the face of music education during the last ten years. In particular, the introduction of the electronic keyboard has meant many more pupils now have access to music making. Keyboards have provided all pupils with the opportunity to perform and compose with a high quality instrument at a reasonable cost, whereas schools would find it difficult to provide instruments and instrumental lessons for all their pupils.

One of the big advantages that technology has brought about is the kudos that it has given to music in schools. It used to be that a certain amount of fun was made, especially of boys who were involved in music, but this is not so today. Technology has bridged the gap and given status and motivation to everyone who is involved with music making. Pupils see the use of music technology in the pop music industry and this has often provided the impetus for their involvement in music making. Pupils can be encouraged to compose music in an idiom of their choice and then move on to all sorts of music making.

Electronic keyboards

Keyboards have developed considerably over recent years. Not so long ago keyboard timbres sounded only roughly like the instruments they represented. The accompaniment styles were very limited and very simple. As technology has advanced the reproduction of timbres has become more convincing and the accompaniment styles have become more complex.

Many more features have been added to keyboards to enhance their potential as a performing and composing instrument. These include touch sensitivity and weighted action which gives the pianist the same feel as a piano action. Memory registration buttons enable the performer to change from one instrument to another very quickly.

Recording facilities

Probably the most important change for education has been the recording facilities that have enabled pupils to play back and edit music that they are composing. Very little music technology is made for the education market. It is mainly made for the home, home recording, semi-professional and professional markets. Education sales are a very small part of a music companies sales and thus it is not viable for them to make equipment specifically for that market.

Initially the recording facilities on keyboards to start with were very limited. At first only a single melody line could be recorded but over the last few years keyboards with eight track sequencers have arrived at a price that most schools can afford. (A sequencer is simply a digital recording device i.e. there is no tape. Eight Tracks signifies that you can record eight different lines of music. A keyboard with the ability to record and have a number of different instruments playing back simultaneously is known as a multi-timbral keyboard.) This development in recording facilities has allowed pupils the facility to record quite complicated pieces of music of their own or make arrangements of other composers compositions.

e.g.	Track 1	Drums
	Track 2	Piano
	Track 3	Strings
	Track 4	Brass
	Track 5	Melody Line

There have been many other advances in music technology that have proved very useful to schools. Four and Eight Track tape recorders, both reel to reel and more recently the cassette version, have proved very popular. It is like having your own mini studio. One person is able to record a piece of music using a number of different instruments so that a complete arrangement of a piece of music can be played back, edited and then mastered on to a normal two track tape machine.

Computers

As technology has advanced drum machines, synthesizers and sequencers have become more common in schools. Synthesizers have developed from quite simple machines to the advanced models that are seen today with very accurate samples of sounds.

The introduction of MIDI (Musical Instrument Digital Interface) has enabled MIDI compatible devices to communicate, sending information from one to the other: keyboard, synthesiser, or drum machine etc.

Computers have also been used to act as sequencers. A MIDI interface can be added to the computer so that it can receive and transmit information to and from another MIDI device, normally a synthesiser. Initially there were very simple packages available from various manufacturers.

The most popular choice now seems to be the IBM PC (and its clones) and quite a lot of software is being produced for them. Steinburg's *Cu Base Score* and its smaller and simpler version, *Cu Base Lite,* seems to be the most popular package available at the moment.

The latest development that is within the scope of most schools is the simple hard disc recording package called *Cu Base Music Station* that can record a live stereo track directly onto the computer's hard disc drive.

Other computers are used for music education. The Archimedes is the most popular in primary schools.

Recording studios

Many schools now have their own mini-recording studio. These vary in complexity from a basic computer and synthesizser to a digital recording studio. This may include a computer, synthesizers, a mixing console, reverb units, graphic equalizers, a sampler, 8 or 16 track digital recorders and a 2 track DAT (Digital Audio Tape) tape machine for mastering purposes.

Hard disc recording (of live instruments) straight onto the computer is the next move forward but an 8 or 16 track hard disc recorder involves gigabytes of memory and a great deal of cash.

Samplers

A sampler is another essential piece of equipment for a good studio.

This allows you to make up sounds of your own, record sounds that you hear and analyse the wave form of the sound. You can then decide how you wish to change the sound, perhaps to create a totally new sound. All these sounds can then be stored on disc and played from another MIDI compatable keyboard. The firms which produce these samplers such as Akai, also have an extensive library of sounds that you can access and record from.

CD-ROM

In the immediate future CD-ROM will also play an important part in the educative process, providing teachers with many resources for teaching the Listening section of the National Curriculum and GCSE. As these discs develop there will be more and more opportunities for analysis of music by pupils as a whole class exercise and at GCSE on a more individual basis. This will give the teacher and the pupil a whole new way of listening to music and hopefully provide increased motivation for pupils to listen to a wide range of music.

John Dempsey is Head of Music at Litherland High School, Sefton, Merseyside. He was a member of a SCAA Advisory Group on the use of IT in music, and has recently been asked to join a DFE Group on the use of IT in music.

CHAPTER SIXTEEN

The Future of IT in Education

Siobhan Wharton

The last ten years have seen an enormous number of changes in the IT industry; the PC has become a commodity item, applications are now largely graphically-based and the overall system specification has improved thousands of times.

The next ten years look like being just as exciting. A number of factors will help to accelerate technological change in education and these can be broken down into three distinct areas:

- there is likely to be wider personal computer ownership
- there will be wider access to information technology
- there could well be increased use and acceptance of Integrated Learning Systems.

Widespread ownership

The average number of computers to pupils is steadily rising in schools but as the price of the hardware continues to fall it seems likely that there will be a marked increase in the number of privately owned computers. More parents will purchase computers for their children.

This could lead to a further increase in the use of IT for curriculum usage as pupils could transport their 'personal workstation' from classroom to classroom and subject to subject, connecting to the school network to use the learning resources provided as required.

Widespread access

New ways of accessing information will arrive over the next decade. With pupils bringing their own notebooks to school they will need a way to connect to the school network and one way of achieving this may be through the use of wireless Local Area Networks (LANs). Wireless LANs operate as a normal network but without the physical wires and connections.

Access to the school's resources need not just come from within the school, pupils could also connect remotely from home. Homework could be carried out at home utilising the school's resources, with the finished work being e-mailed back to the teacher ready to collect in the morning.

Remote access need not stop at accessing the school's facilities. Pupils and teachers could gain access to other schools, libraries, museums, commercial organisations and even television and radio stations. These could be in the same town or country or even over-seas. The information collected can then be incorporated into relevant project work.

Integrated Learning Systems

Integrated Learning Systems are sophisticated courseware packages that allow teachers to assign pupils specific tasks or sequences of lessons whilst monitoring their performance and storing data for producing performance reports. Today in America, schools spend over $300 million on such systems and research data suggests that the American ILS market will grow to over $400 million by 1998.

Such systems range from simple 'drill and practice' packages, which require constant manual teacher adjustment, to very large systems which can automatically individualise the material according to the responses of each pupil - this provides a degree of differentiation which is hard to match in any other way. Integrated Learning Systems often include basic skills material, but are now also being extended to include open-ended experiences such as simulation and exploratory activities, combining basic skills development with problem-solving and higher order thinking skills. It is likely that over the next ten years these systems will evolve to offer open-ended experiences such as simulations and exploratory activities, combining basic skill development with problem solving and higher-order thinking skills.

Technology in education: the need for change

Experts have predicted that 80% of the jobs that will be available by the year 2000 do not exist today and therefore schools will undoubt-edly need to adjust to these new demands. The technology is, and will increasingly be there for schools to exploit and it is up to schools to use and control this technology to shape the school of the future.

Siobhan Wharton works for Research Machines plc and may be contacted at New Mill House, 183 Milton Park, Abingdon, Oxon OX14 4SE.

hospitalisation